EXTRACTS

FROM

THE RELIGIOUS WORKS

OF

FENELON

TRANSLATED FROM THE ORIGINAL FRENCH

BY

LOUISA A. MARSHALL

This book is a reprint of

Extracts from the Religious Works of La Mothe Fenelon, Archbishop of Cambray

Translated from the original French
by Louisa A. Marshall
London: Printed for John Hatchard and Son, 1823.

ISBN:0615767753
ISBN-13:9780615767758

This book is Volume 4 of
Our Christian Heritage Foundation's
Historical Reprints Series

Also available from Our Christian Heritage Foundation:

The Religion that Shaped America, Dr. Byron Perrine, Editor

Emerson's Evangelical Primer,
Vol. 1 of Our Christian Heritage Foundation's
Historical Reprints Series

Memoir of Catharine Brown—A Christian Indian of the
Cherokee Nation, by Rufus Anderson, Vol. 2 of Our Christian
Heritage Foundation's Historical Reprints Series

Christian Unity 101, Dr. Byron Perrine, W. Harness and
Baptist Wriothesley Noel, Vol. 3 of Our Christian Heritage
Foundation's Historical Reprints Series

CONTENTS

CHAPTER 1.
ON OUR REDEMPTION THROUGH CHRIST, AND THE FAITH WHICH IT REQUIRES FROM US

How wonderful, how sublime, are the thoughts which fill the mind of a Christian, when he reflects on the great mystery of our Redemption, set forth to us in the life and sufferings of our Redeemer! When he sees that God so loved the world, that while we were yet in our sins, while we were grieving his Holy Spirit, even then, God sent his only Son, the Prince of Peace, the Lord of Glory, to suffer for us; to expiate our crimes by submitting to the punishment due to them. How infinite the mercy, how unspeakable the love of our gracious Savior, thus willingly to offer himself for us; to become the victim of the wrath of the Almighty! Let us for a moment consider the doom to which the justice of our Creator must have adjudged us forever, without the interposition of Jesus Christ; "who, by the sacrifice of himself, once offered," became a full, perfect, and sufficient sacrifice, oblation, and satisfaction for the sins of the whole world, not of a single generation, but of all who should faithfully believe his mission, and receive his holy Gospel, to the end of time. Let us consider also, that the efficacy of this sacrifice is perpetuated by an express institution: for the Savior has left to us miserable sinners, the means of remembering this great mercy, and preserving in our souls the due gratitude for it, in the sacrament of the Lord's Supper—"Do this in remembrance of me."

In meditating on the great and wonderful subject of our Redemption, of God manifested in the flesh, it is not necessary that we should perplex our minds with examining those high mysteries of our faith, which we cannot comprehend. They are to be believed on account of the divine testimony which attends them, but they are not proposed as rules of our conduct in this world; neither is the comprehension of them necessary to our salvation in the next. We have abundant subjects of meditation in the works and ways of our Creator, which are plain and easy to the lowest capacity; and the rules and precepts of the Gospel are so clear and simple, that our reflections on them can never prove embarrassing or perplexing to us: and in examining and meditation on these rules and precepts, we are to take especial care that our conviction of their truth be always followed by our sincere practice of them, to the utmost of our power. For, to disregard the truth, to resist the grace of God (that is, willfully to neglect the Gospel, when we are once convinced of its divine origin and obligation), is the sin against the Holy Ghost, mentioned in Scripture as the most dreadful of all sins, and that which God will not pardon.

Are our minds tormented with doubts and distrust of the truth and reality of God's word? And because some of the great mysteries of our religion are beyond our comprehension, do we therefore refuse them our belief?

Let us remember that we are not commanded to comprehend them, but only to believe. Let us not presume to subject to our reason that which reason cannot explain. The mysteries and obscurities of our faith, are indeed very different from a state of doubt and distrust. Is our faith accompanied with any uneasiness to our minds? We have the consolation of being in a state of security, while we obey God's commands. Doubts of the truth of Revelation, are the troubles of a soul without a resting-place, desirous of discovering what God has seen fit to conceal. What have you to sacrifice to God but your own opinion, and your self-love? Would you pretend to virtue, and yet forfeit the first step in your duty—an implicit reliance on God for everything? Would you have God, the incomprehensible, the infinite God, subject himself to the limited faculties of the creature whom he has made? Abraham believed God, and it was imputed unto him for righteousness. He hesitated not to offer up his only son a sacrifice to the command of God, though he could not comprehend the fitness of such command. And what reward can we expect for our belief, it we require miracles to assure us of the truth of his Word?—Our Savior says, "Blessed are they who have not seen, and yet have believed." If we believe in one Almighty God, we must necessarily believe all and every part of that which he has revealed to us.

The Gospel tells us, that Jesus Christ is the true Light, which enlighteneth every man that cometh into the world. As there is but one sun to give light to the material world, so there is but one Light, on Spirit to direct the soul of man; even the Word of Jesus Christ. This is the eternal Word, the Light of Truth; without it, we are blind and foolish; and unless we permit it to shine upon us, we remain in darkness: every other light which ariseth among us, is false and deceitful; it is vain, and unworthy of our confidence.

How blind, then, are all those who think themselves wise, if they are not filled with the wisdom of Jesus Christ! They wander in a think darkness, after unreal phantoms; they find their own misery in so doing, and yet they still follow that which leads them astray: "hungry and thirsty, their souls faint in them;" yet they will not "cry unto the Lord, who alone can deliver them out of their distress." The world, by which they are intoxicated, causes them a sorrow, far greater than any pleasure it can ever bestow; yet they will not cease to follow after its vanities, and to make its false maxims their oracles. They look upon all those who are in the clear light of the Gospel as fools; the grace of God appears to them as a vain dream; they can no more comprehend it, than a blind man, who never saw the sun, can comprehend the nature of its rays: but as that glorious luminary dispenses light and heat to the whole world, so does the grace of God display itself to all, who will with their whole heart seek after Jesus.

The Gospel, indeed, is read and preached in all Christian countries, and Christians say that they believe in its doctrines; but do they follow, and act up to its precepts? Do they obey its laws? How many, who call themselves Christians, rest satisfied with the name, without ever considering how unworthy they are of bearing it. They pass this short life in a profound slumber, or a visionary dream: but the time will come when they shall be aroused indeed! They shall awaken on a dreadful day, when eternity will at once appear before them; and the light of Jesus, so long contemned, shall shine around them, but shall shine only to strike and dazzle their astonished eyes. The world, that world in which alone they trusted, shall vanish from them like smoke; all its pomps and vanities shall crumble away like dust, from those who placed in them their foolish confidence; all its splendors shall be laid low; its power shall be broken, and its pride crushed, beneath the feet of the insulted Majesty, and Supreme Power of the eternal God, who will then manifest himself in awful wrath and terrible glory, to those who have rejected him. How dreadful will this day be to you, if you now you're your eyes to that Light, which is offered for your safe conduct through this life! Seek not to deceive yourself; as surely as night follows day in this life, so surely a day of retribution and of judgment will follow death. The votaries of the world, and of its sinful pleasures, will then call on it in vain; in vain will they cry to those objects in which alone they trusted: alas! They shall not find even a trace of them left behind. This world, which now seems so secure to them, will then have passed away (as the shadows of night flee before the rising sun), and the place thereof shall know it no more. O world! So weak, so vain, what art thou but a dream? And shall I put my trust in thee; when I feel that even the enjoyment of thy most tempting pleasures leaves nothing but emptiness and vanity behind? Art thou not ashamed, O world, to deck with magnificent and splendid titles, the miseries with which thou leadest us astray? Alas, at the moment thou appearest to us most lovely, thou lurest us to destruction! In one hand is thy sparkling cup, in the other thy poisoned dagger.—Away from me, vain world! I will put my trust in my God, and walk in the light of my

Redeemer Jesus Christ.

O, thou great and glorious Almighty and incomprehensible Being, give me grace to lift my feeble and erring thoughts to Thee. How can I presume to understand Thee, when this world, and all its wonders, are but the smallest part of thy works? Creator Infinite! Thou has made my heart; let it be always devoted to thy service; and as it is from Thee that every good thought proceeds, fill my soul, O God, with thy grace, and let me ever love and serve Thee. Amen.

Oh, strange perversion of human reason that, instead of humbling ourselves at the throne of our offended Creator, and thankfully acknowledging the unspeakable love and pity of our Savior, we should dare madly to doubt the revelation of his Word, and scornfully to reject the offered terms of salvation! Let the unbelieving sinner awake, before the justice of God cut him off in the midst of his offences. Then it will be too late to call upon the glorious Redeemer, whom he has despised; and his portion shall be fixed to all eternity, in that dreadful place, where the fire shall not be quenched, and where shall be weeping and gnashing of teeth.

What must we do to be saved? We must renounce ourselves, our passions, our worldly interests, as far as they are at variance with the laws of God. We must devote our lives to his service, and have no will, no wish, no hope, but in his love and approbation: in that alone is our rest in this life; and that alone can enable us to look with hope and confidence to the life to come.

But, O Lord God, how shall a vile sinner dare to know his Creator? How shall a creature of the dust, the work of they hands, presume to look up to the Maker of the universe? How shall he hope for pardon from an all-perfect Being, who cannot behold sin without abhorrence? Where shall we wretched sons of mortality find hope, but in the mediation and all-sufficient merits of their Redeemer?—Yes; in Jesus Christ we may securely hope. There is no sin which does not leave to us the privilege of repentance; and from repentance our blessed Savior will never turn away. His place is at the right hand of God, where he ever liveth to make intercession for us

God created the first man pure and free from sin; free to have continued so; but man yielded to temptation, and fell from his original righteousness. So great was the abhorrence of God for sin, that the punishment of it was death; nor could the sinner escape the bitter penalty, unless some way should be found to satisfy the offended justice of God. Mankind had debased themselves in his sight, and were no longer worthy to be called his children. What, then, must have become of them, thus lost forever; had not his mercy, his infinite and unspeakable mercy, interposed in their behalf, by the propitiation of our Savior Jesus Christ? By giving himself up in our stead, he has made atonement for the sins of the whole world:--"He became sin for us, that we might become the righteousness of God in Him." By his death he has destroyed death; and by his rising to life again, restored to all who believe in him, everlasting life.

Let us, then, stifle in our hearts whatever doubts may arise in us, tending to weaken our faith in the promises of God, and our implicit reliance on his mercy and justice towards mankind. God made man, we are told, in his own image; free from sin, and pure in his sight. His bountiful Creator then placed him in a delightful abode, and set before him good and evil; the one to conduct him to eternal happiness; the other consigning him to death, the inevitable punishment of his transgressions. Thus was he forewarned, thus sufficient to have stood: and the *freedom of the will of man* was the necessary consequence of that gift of reason, which distinguished him from the brute creation. In his fall, therefore, whom can he accuse with justice but himself?—Not his Maker; for God had given him sufficient powers of resistance.— Not the Tempter; for of what value is that virtue which has never been tried?—Indeed, we have only the doubts and assertions of man against this statement; and we cannot but confess the justice of the Almighty, in the punishment of a creature whom he himself had made, although he foreknew how soon that creature was to fall from a state of such felicity in Paradise, to that of misery, which is the portion of man since his expulsion from it.

We have innumerable and incontestable proofs of the truth and wisdom of God in the creation, as it is recorded in the Holy Scriptures. If we then willfully reject the Word of God, and...refuse to receive our blessed Redeemer, we are obstinately blind; and therefore guilty of incurring our own everlasting punishment.

O, my God, it is enough! Henceforth be far from me the abuse of thy gift of reason, in daring to doubt or question thy ways. Grant me the grace of thy Holy Spirit, that in silence I may believe and adore. O, Father of Mercy, banish from my mind all tormenting doubts and difficulties; more especially this: Why thou has created human beings, whose end will be never-ceasing misery?—Why thou has given thine only Son to die as the Redeemer of the world, though his precious death will save but few, in comparison of those who will perish through their unbelief? Oh! Let me know, and ever hold fast the saving truth that thou art God, and that therefore all thy works and ways must be right, although some of them are far beyond the comprehension of man; and that thy glory is perfected in those who are saved, as is thy justice in those who perish. "God hateth nothing that he hath made; he desireth not the death of a sinner, but rather that he should turn from his wickedness and live." Were God, therefore, now to enter into judgment with the world, the condemned sinner could not complain; "the judgment of God would stand forever, and be done in truth and equity;" since it would plainly appear that God had done everything "for the vine which he had planted; but that the ungrateful tree, which he had nurtured, instead of its proper fruit, had brought forth wild grapes."

Mankind do not consider how they provoke their Maker by accusing him of having done too little for them; whereas, would they but estimate themselves justly, they would perceive that they are not worthy of the least of all his mercies; not worthy of being called his children. If God foreknew, he did not therefore ordain their fall. Their Maker left them free,—and on their own heads be their punishment.

O Lord, my God! When I consider all this, how fearful are the thoughts of my soul! Look upon me, O my God! Fashion my spirit to obey they will! Enter into my soul, and restore me to thy divine image, from which I am so greatly fallen!—I desire to devote myself unto Thee: I receive with joy and hope thy holy Gospel, and the terms and promises of salvation, through my blessed Redeemer. With humble confidence I will trust in Thee, O Lord: be it unto me according to thy Word. Amen.

CHAPTER 2.
ADVICES AND REFLECTIONS ON HUMILITY, AND THE LOVE OF GOD

Be not discouraged by your sins; there is a way to bear them, without cherishing them, and of coercing them without impatience: seek this of God (with an entire distrust of yourself), and you will find it. We are strong in God when we are weak in ourselves, and confess our sins.

The love of God (far from being a burden) will make our labors light; and if we perform our duties through that principle only, they will be both pleasant and comfortable; for, however great the sacrifices, or painful the trials which may accompany them; yet, if these are submitted to through the love of God, they will prove easy and profitable to us.

Our sins, our infirmities, and, of course, our trials, arise from the indulgence of our passions it is only the fear of God, and the divine love of Him, that can enable us to endure our own afflictions, or to rise superior to the evils which may be brought on us by others.

Nothing can be so good, so tender, so gentle, so

amiable, as a heart filled with the love of God. In religion there is nothing gloomy or severe; it enlarges the heart, and warms the affections; but it does not consist in a set form of words, or a scrupulous observance of outward ceremonies: a truly religious disposition shows itself in performance of the duties and virtues which belong to our peculiar situations in the world. If we make it our constant endeavor to serve God to the utmost of our power, and to improve our time, we shall have our minds at peace; our hearts will be purified; we shall have piety without scruple, and happiness without alloy.

Who in this world is free from sin? Who is just in the sight of God? Yet let us not despair; it is in our own power to abhor and strive against our sins; and God requires no more.

The noblest victory is that which we obtain over ourselves; and the greatest courage consists in not being overcome by our misfortunes. Let us then try to perform our duties with simplicity and steadiness; the fear of God, and the belief of his constant presence, will enable us on all occasions to decide what we should do in this world. We should, therefore, often enter into ourselves, and by the examination of our hearts, refresh, and strengthen in them the love of God. If we do but sincerely endeavor to live for him, and to be faithful to his laws, he will never forsake us. Every advance which we make in the path of goodness, will be an increase of peace and comfort to our souls. What greater happiness can we desire, than to have our minds always at ease? This content we can find only in subduing our passions, and submitting ourselves to the will of the Almighty.

Our minds, our feelings, must have some object; life becomes insupportable when we have not something to love. But if this object be not virtue, what is to become of us? The most debased and foolish passions which possess us, arise from attachments wrongly placed. God created us to love him and to obey him; and if we pervert our natural love of virtue by our passions, we frustrate the end of our creation. Since, therefore, we must love something, let us reflect well before we prefer the folly, the insincerity, and the hypocrisy of the world, to the divine satisfaction of loving God, whose end in creating us was our happiness here and hereafter. Let us see this world as it is, a thing incapable of satisfying a being destined for eternity. Love and serve God, therefore, to the utmost of your power, and strive to conquer your passions; he can, and will reward you, perhaps in this world, but most assuredly in the world to come.

How can we reflect for a moment, and be guilty of the dreadful crime of resisting the grace of God in our hearts, and willfully shutting our eyes against the truths of his Gospel? There are few who have not experienced the ingratitude and unworthiness of the world; few who will not own how illusive is the bliss which it bestows upon its votaries. Can we then, for its fleeting momentary pleasures, exchange the hopes of eternity and the joys of heaven? None of us can really doubt that we were created by God, and that the universe is the work of his power: how much more criminal then are men, in behaving with ingratitude to their Creator, than to one another? Yet, though forgetful of the divine goodness to ourselves, we are ready to exclaim against society, and to condemn our fellow-creatures, when we meet with ingratitude from them.

We can have no assurance that the love of God exists in our hearts, but by the conformity oif our lives to the rules and precepts of the Gospel. Let us be satisfied with the light that shines upon us, without vainly scrutinizing, or presumptuously doubting, the truth of that light; and since we know not the day nor the hour when we shall be called upon to give an account of the work we may have done, let us prepare ourselves while yet we have time. Self-love produces in us doubts, envy, revenge, distrust, and an uncharitable disposition; than which nothing can be more removed from the love of God, and more opposite to that blessed, peaceful, humble, resigned, and contented disposition and frame of mind, which is the certain portion of a heart that sincerely feels the true love of God.

Jesus Christ has left us true riches in leaving us this poverty; but we impoverish ourselves in our eager pursuits after worldly good. We may have nothing, and yet possess all things. Whatever we forego or resign for the love God, he will make up to us, in that peace and comfort to our souls which ever attend the sacrifice.

When we have made any progress in goodness and the service of God, we are too much inclined to fall into a state of negligent security, and to imagine that we are steadfast and immovable, forgetting the words of our blessed Lord, "Watch and pray, lest ye enter into temptation." And thus, instead of daily becoming more zealous for God's service, and more perfect in our duty, we content ourselves with not falling into the commission of any heinous sins: but in not making constant us of our means of salvation to the utmost of our power, we are as faulty as those, who, perhaps for want of such means, are guilty of more serious crimes. And further, we provoke God to withdraw his Holy Spirit from us, by our ingratitude for it, and our neglect of its suggestions.

We should constantly strive, without loitering or carelessness, to advance in that path which we shall never be permitted to retrace, with watchfulness and humility, since we can have no security for our continuing in it, nor any knowledge of the hour when we shall be summoned before our Creator, to give an account of the manner in which we shall have performed our journey here.

We must carefully beware of that presumption which too often overrates our virtues, and the performance of our duties. Our Lord Jesus Christ, who knew his disciples better than they did themselves, told them, that they were not able, in their present state, to bear all that he had to say to them. And when he was entering on his Passion and Cross, he said, that in that very night they would all be ashamed of him, that one of them would betray, and another deny him. St. Peter (to whom our Lord here alluded) replied that, "Though he should die with him, he would not deny him in any wise:" but Jesus, who knew his weakness and presumption, told him, that before a few hours should pass, he would be capable of affirming that he had never seen him; and we find that the simple assertion of a servant-maid was enough to make him forswear his Lord and Master. If, then, so good a man as St. Peter could so mistake and misjudge himself, how watchful should we be against religious presumption and security!

Insert chapter two text Let us be content to live a humble and obscure life, if such be the will of God; and if he has so placed us in this world, let us bear our daily crosses and vexations with an even temper and a quiet mind: they are (no doubt) good for us, and we have need of them; they are the merciful exercises of God to our souls. We cannot live unto righteousness, but by dying continually unto the world and unto sin.

We should make it a rule frequently to look into ourselves, and to examine our conscience, with a heart disengaged from the flatteries, and free from the prejudices of self-love, that we may learn to know ourselves, and faithfully to call upon God for his grace to correct our sins. And when God, by his grace, enables us to perceive our faults, and to become acquainted with our imperfections, it is then more especially our duty to amend them to the utmost of our power. We must resign every sinful pleasure, and even the excess of every tender affection (whatever we may suffer in so doing), and conform ourselves wholly to the laws and rules of the Gospel.

When we thus, in earnest, open our hearts to the grace of God, we shall discover, even in our best works, a thousand sinful imperfections and infirmities, which continually call for the inexhaustible goodness of God.

We are truly humble when we allow others to discover faults in us, which we are not willing to own to ourselves, and when we receive their rebukes and corrections with patience and a sincere desire to profit by them. Self-love conceals from our view many of our frailties; and while we indulge this passion, we cannot but be surprised that they should be discovered in us by our fellow-creatures: but true humility will make us distrust and think lowly of ourselves: it will also make us turn to God for his grace to conquer our evil dispositions; and then, even the corrections of our fellow-creatures (however severe) will appear no more than we deserve.

Self-love prevents us from knowing ourselves; indeed

we could not bear to see the real state of our souls, tainted as they are with the corruptions of the world. Our shame would be too great, and despair would take possession of our hearts, were it not that a resting-place is afforded us by the infinite mercy of God, through faith and trust in the all-sufficient merits and mediation of our blessed Redeemer Jesus Christ. Let us endeavor, therefore, by degrees to root up our self-love. In its stead let us place the love of God in our hearts; we shall then have courage to look into ourselves, and whatever imperfections we there may find, we shall not despair; we shall only pray more earnestly for the grace of God, that we may be enabled to work out our salvation, and humbly look forward to that blessed state in which our souls shall be purified through the merits of our Savior, and our sinful bodies shall be washed with his most precious blood; when we shall dwell in him, and he in us, in the presence of the Creator, and exist in the adoration of his perfections to all eternity.

Let us consider, for a moment, how different are the lives of the generality of Christians (even the best of them) from that of our blessed Lord. At his birth he was laid in a manger; he passed thirty years in the labors of common life; he suffered hunger, and thirst, and fatigue; he was poor and humble; he preached the way of life, and taught the doctrine of peace and salvation: yet he was despised and rejected: the rich and great men of his nation persecuted him; they not only condemned him to a most painful and shameful death (although he was innocent), but basely scourged him, and, in derision, crowned him with thorns. He was mocked and despitefully used, and at last was put to death between two malefactors. Such was the life that Jesus Christ, the

Son of God, led on earth, and such the pains he endured for us; and shall we not humble ourselves before God, and take our necks from the yoke of sin? Let us compare our lives with that of Jesus, and let us remember that he is our Master, and we his servants; that he is the all-powerful God, and we but poor, weak, sinful mortals; yet he humbled and abased himself, and we are continually exalting and puffing ourselves up with the vanities of the world. O, miserable sinners! If we would search our own hearts, we should find ample cause for humility; we should, with prayer and supplication, turn to Him, who alone hath the words of eternal life. And how are we to turn to him, if we do not endeavor to imitate him (as far as we are able), both in the excellency of his life, and the purity of his character, in his patience and humility under persecution and contempt, in his gentleness and long-suffering, his pity for the misfortunes and sorrows of others, and even for their sins? Jesus Christ quitted the right hand of God, and the joys of heaven, where he was the Lord of glory, the Ruler of angels, and the beloved Son of God himself; to live in this manner on earth, and to suffer a dreadful death, for no other end but our good, and our eternal happiness. To this great privilege, which has been so dearly purchased for us, we can have no claim, unless we follow his example, and conform ourselves to his holy life. To be Christians, is to be followers of Jesus; therefore, to imitate him in his patience and resignation, his humility and self-denial, is the only way to follow him. He is God as well as man; and as he is all-powerful, we must adore him; as just, we fear him; as merciful and gracious, we must love him with all our soul, and with all our strength; but in his humility, his patience, his resignation, his submission and lowliness, we must follow and imitate him. Nor yet are we presumptuously to suppose that even this imitation of our blessed Lord is to come from ourselves alone; "in our flesh dwelleth no good thing:" but Jesus Christ is a merciful Lord, he knoweth our infirmities, for he was in all things like unto us, though without sin. He has promised, therefore (and he is faithful and just), an abundant measure of his Holy Spirit, and his Almighty assistance, to those who sincerely pray for it.

There is no virtue more constantly inculcated in the Gospel than humility, nor any which is more acceptable in the sight of God. Our Savior himself tells us, "that God giveth grace to the humble." Humility is not only a virtue in ourselves, but its effects prove a blessing to others. The view of our own faults and sufferings, renders us indulgent and compassionate to our fellow creatures: it affords us also abundant causes for humbling ourselves before God; for we cannot think, without the deepest self-abasement, on the miserable and despairing condition from which the mercy and the power of God have raised us. Indeed, it is only by accustoming ourselves continually to think of God, and by loving him with all our soul and with all our strength, that we can conquer our pride and vain-glory, and attain that meek and quiet spirit, "which is, in the sight of God, of great price." If we truly love God, we must abhor and detest ourselves; and when we do so, our greatest faults and errors may be turned to our good, by thus making them the causes of our humility; and we may, through faith and trust in our blessed Savior, certainly hope for the pardon of them. But this humbling sense of our own unworthiness is not meant to lead our minds to despair and carelessness of amendment: that is a very sinful frame of mind, and will never bring us to any good. Let us make us of past sins and errors to produce that fear and distrust of ourselves which is ever the companion of true humility, and an incitement to virtue. Despair never yet answered any good purpose, and in this case it is, in fact, only our wounded self-love. The true way to profit by this humiliating sense of our faults is to look upon them in all their turpitude, to detest and abhor ourselves for them, but not to lose our hope and trust in the mercy of God. To entertain this just sense of our faults without despair, and to avoid the presumptuous supposition that we are faultless, is the temper of mind which we ought to cultivate as the true and spiritual state of a Christian.

We often meet with a kind of humility which avows itself unworthy of the mercy of God, and therefore will not apply to him for it, and which founds a plea for continuing in a state of sin, upon the idea that repentance will avail us nothing. This is not Christian humility, but a reprobate and wicked state of mind. God is ever more ready to hear than we to pray; and we know that our Savior came into the world to call, "not the righteous, but sinners to repentance."

Religion, in a great measure, consists in renouncing ourselves, in combating our self-love, and resigning all to God. The pure love of God consists in our will; the great our humility, and the more implicit and unhesitating our acquiescence in the will of God, the nearer we approach to that virtue and that love of him which he demands of us.

The strong truths of religion make it a terror to weak minds; but the reason of this is, that they do not properly understand it. They know not what it gives, and what it promises, so that to them it appears a system of severe and painful sacrifices, of gloomy and sorrowful practice. They will not understand that bond of love between the Creator and his creatures, which is the very essence of religion, and which makes easy all the duty which it requires. Those who possess the true love of God are at all times cheerful and happy; they find that the yoke of Jesus is easy, and his burden light; they find that he gives rest unto their souls, and that he refreshes all those who are weary and heavy-laden with the burden of this life. But those divine words of our Lord can afford no comfort to those cowardly and debased souls, which cannot shake off the dominion of the world, and renounce the service of the devil. God's holy service, his supporting grace, and his refreshing comforts, are incompatible with a life devoted to the world, and to the slavery of sin. You must either give your heart to God, or to the world; you can make no reserves with your duty; the first commandment of the Law most clearly points out to us what God requires:—"Thou shalt love the Lord thy God with all thy mind and with all thy strength." How then can they pretend to love God, or to serve him, who do not love him above all things? And what effect should our love of God have, but that of keeping his commandments? Those who call themselves Christians, and yet obey the laws which Christ has set before them, only when they find it conducing to their own pleasure or profit, resemble the multitude which followed Jesus, not for his doctrine, but "because they did eat of the loaves and fishes, and were filled." To such we may attribute the speech of St. Peter, "Lord, it is good for us to be here, and let us build here three tabernacles for ourselves;" but, like St. Peter, they know not what they say. They are willing to be the disciples of Christ on Mount Tabor, but they will not follow him to Calvary. Those only are truly his disciples, who are always ready to accompany their Lord "to prison and to death," and this in defiance of the world, the flesh, and the devil.

The more humble and docile your soul becomes, and the more unresistingly it follows the calls of the Holy Spirit, the greater is its progress in simplicity; not that it becomes blind to its own faults, and unconscious of its infirmities; it feels them with redoubled force, it regards them with horror; the knowledge of its own sinfulness increases every day, but it does not arrive at that knowledge through pride, vanity, or self-love; it discovers its own faults by comparing itself with the perfections of its Creator: thus it is free in its course, it goes on with its God, singly and uprightly, without turning our of the way for the profits or allurements which sin offers. It thinks more of God than of anything which he has created. It has no vain and self-approving reflections, neither does it give way to any dejecting scruples about its own condition, which so often produce, on weak minds, superstition and melancholy, and in those which are stronger, a presumptuous confidence incompatible with the love of God.

Nor do we require much time to cultivate the love of God in our souls; nor will it cost us any great pains. On the contrary, we shall find this duty easy and delightful, if we only make it our constant thought and remembrance that we are ever in his sight. Lift up your heart continually, and on all occasions, towards him; adore him in the sincerity of your soul, and resign all you have to him:—This state will raise us above the troubles of the world. If, however, the importunity of our senses, or the vivacity of our imagination, should injure or impede this state of recollection, and the constant resignation of our souls to God; yet we must still be careful to keep up in ourselves the wish of acquiring such a frame of mind. If this is sincere in us, God will accept it, and he will pardon our involuntary wanderings, when we really and truly lament them, and endeavor with all our heart to renew, from time to time, the desire of wholly resigning ourselves to God, of knowing him better, of obeying more perfectly his commandments, and of loving him above all things.

When worldly objects give us too much pleasure, let us pause and remember that the heart is not to be given to them: —"My son, give God thine heart," is a precept which we have from God himself: and if we faithfully endeavor to prevent any object (how dear soever it may be to us) from usurping that power over our souls which should belong to God alone, we shall feel that pure joy, that holy and celestial calm, which God never fails to bestow on the heart devoted to him. When we feel a passionate desire towards anything, or action (whatever it may be), if only to speak a word, to approach a place, or to look upon an object, we should check ourselves, and examine our motive; and however innocent or trifling the action may appear, yet we should consider it well before we surrender our will, and endeavor to calm that too eager and tumultuous wish, which, if indulged on trivial occasions, will acquire power to lead us astray in matters of greater consequence. And remember, that the divine grace and Holy Spirit of God will never dwell with unrestrained and unsubdued passions.

The true sense of these words of our blessed Savior, "Whosoever will be my disciple, let him deny himself, and take up his cross and follow me," is this, that we renounce our own will, and give it up entirely to Christ; not making a path of our own to walk in, but following Christ implicitly wherever he has vouchsafed to lead the way. Let us, therefore, beseech the God of mercies, the Father of consolation, that he will incline our hearts to his love, and bow our wills to his service; and that, when oiur weak and frail nature revolts against him, he will not turn away from us, but vouchsafe to us the grace and assistance of his Holy Spirit; that the sense of our past errors may humble us in our own eyes, without discouraging us in the performance of our duty.

Let us, therefore, humbly lean upon our God; let us turn to him for support. Aided by him, we need not fear our own weakness. This is the only way, by which we can endure the humiliating sense of our corrupt nature. We shall not then despair at the view of our continual errors; we shall sorrow for them; but we shall learn to give glory to God, for the assistance which he offers to us, and acknowledge that, without it, we are helpless and miserable. We must, therefore, pray to God, to take from our hearts all presumptuous confidence in ourselves, on one hand, and all desponding and enervating fear of him on the other. Let us beseech him to strengthen us with the grace of his Holy Spirit, that we may be able to comprehend the Christian mystery; let us beseech him, that being of the communion of saints, we may follow their holy example on earth, and that, when we die, we may be admitted to their blessed fellowship in heaven.

CHAPTER 3.
THOUGHTS ON THE GOODNESS OF GOD; HIS PROVIDENCE AND JUSTICE IN THE GOVERNMENT OF THIS WORLD; AND THE TRUST AND OBEDIENCE WHICH HE HAS A RIGHT TO REQUIRE OF US

Mankind often accuse Providence, and question the Wisdom, as well as the Justice of God, in the government and regulation of the affairs of this world; and even good men are grieved, and know not what to say to those who thus murmur against their Creator, when they behold vice and immorality prosperous and triumphant, and virtue so often trampled upon and oppressed. The wicked almost tempt them to believe that God does not regard what passes in the world: but, O, ye righteous, hold fast your integrity, and be patient! Impiety may triumph for a time, and wickedness may flourish in the earth; but it will not endure: at the blasting of the breath of God's displeasure, it will fade away, and perish as the grass of the field; which in the morning is green and growth up, but in the evening is cut down, dried up, and withered. Death comes to the just and to the unjust, and is equally the end of all men. It reduces all conditions to the same level, as to the goods of this world; for, as man brought nothing with him into life, so neither can he carry anything out of it.—Yet a little while, O man, and thou shalt behold the Almighty coming to judge the world, and to render unto every one according to his works! Let not, then, the wicked exult in his prosperity, and say, Why should I fear, since the end of these things is far off?—Alas, it is but too near for him: the hour is coming, when the good and bad shall be forever separated; their eternal state shall commence, and to each of them shall be given his portion forever!

When we feel doubts of the Divine Being, or distrust of his Providence, arising in our hearts, let us not be discouraged; these are to be accounted the suggestions of our great enemy, the devil, who is continually on the watch to lead us astray. Let us, therefore, not open our minds to them. We know what God requires of us, and what we must do to be saved: let us do it, then; and, in an implicit obedience to his commands, and submission to his will, we shall find peace; "for, who hath hardened himself against God, and prospered?" If we will but taste and see how gracious the Lord is, we shall have no desire to forsake his laws, or to turn aside from the duties which he hath set before us.

The knowledge which is most necessary to mankind, is that in which they are generally most deficient; and it is not till after much study, that they become acquainted with the wonders and dispensations of Providence. From the facts of History, they may draw many serious and profound reflections on the corruption and inconstancy of the world; they may be convinced of the utility of certain rules and maxims, for the maintenance of good order and morality: but of what avail is all their knowledge, unless it leads them to their Creator, and to the hopes of their own salvation?—Belief in God, and the practice of virtue, through his love and fear, is the one thing needful to the good Christian, the moving-spring of whose every action should be, the persuasion that one All-powerful God is over all; —that everything proceeds from him, and is ordered for the best; —that he is the Creator and Ruler of all things; infinite in power, immutable in wisdom, and unbounded in love and mercy; —that his works are as far above our comprehension, as the heavens are above the earth; —that the operation of his Will is as full and perfect in the least of the works of Nature, as in the greatest—in the lowest reptile that crawls on the earth, as in the glorious Archangel, who worships in ecstasy before his throne; —that the Power of the Almighty is in his Will, and that his Will is unbounded and unrestrained. He could create another universe with the same ease with which he causes his thunder to roll, or his rain to descend. His love, mercy, and long-suffering towards his poor sinful creatures, are as infinite in their operations as even his Wisdom and Power. From him proceed all the comforts and blessings we enjoy in this world; and he has prepared an eternity of joys unspeakable, for all who will believe in him, and serve him. Nor is that service hard, nor is God a severe master. What can be easier than to adore Supreme Perfection, and to obey laws framed for our own happiness, both in this world and in the world to come? His Justice towards the impenitent, and his Mercy to the repenting sinner, have, each of them, their source in his perfections. He forgives, that he may fulfill his everlasting promise; —he punishes, that he may vindicate the offended sanctity of his laws.

In God alone, therefore, can we have hope or comfort: dreadful is the present, still more dreadful will be the future state of those who do not rest on him. It is from his Love that we derive existence; for the Power which hath created us for happiness (if it be not our own fault) might have denied us being, had it so pleased: yet our frail and finite knowledge would degrade our Creator to the standard of our own miserable conceptions; and because we cannot comprehend, we refuse to believe and obey.

We are told in Scripture, that God hath made all things for himself, and to contribute to his own glory. Man, therefore, the principal of his works (as far as the Creator has thought fit to reveal them), is unquestionably his; and he has an undoubted right to dispose of what he has made, as may please him. God certainly desires our happiness, because it is agreeable to the attribute of his goodness to desire it. To those only, who make God their constant study, and whose constant hope it is to attain the requisite degree of perfection, is it given to comprehend man, and all creation, as existing and contributing to the glory of the Creator. Self-love is ever supposing that *our* happiness, and *our* concerns, are the *first* objects of God's care: but it was another principle which dictated those words of the Apostle, "Whether we live, we live unto the Lord; or whether we die, we die unto the Lord; so that living or dying, we are his only."

We fear to examine the truths of the Gospel, lest we should find them too strong to resist. We first presume to doubt them, and then we endeavor to persuade ourselves, that since we doubt, we ought not to take any step towards God, lest we fall into error, and be deceived in our belief. It is not, however, that in reality we doubt the truth of the Gospel Revelation, for then we should willingly endeavor to be convinced; but we make use of this pretense for continuing in our sins, and giving ourselves up to the world. But we do not know the consolations of Religion when we argue in this manner. We look upon the gratifications of sin, which it forbids to us in this world, without thinking of those joys which it promises in the next. We exaggerate our present sacrifices, without considering the inability of this world to make us happy; were it sufficient to do so, it would be a better master than it is. Religion, by subliming our ideas, renders us superior to the disappointments of the world, and leaves no void in our hearts. Our Savior came into the world to call sinners to repentance; and, for his sake, God will bear with us. He will prepare our minds by his grace, and soften our hearts by his love, if we will only turn to him: we do not deserve the patience, the long-suffering, which he shows towards us. Let us not dare, then, to doubt our Creator, but let us distrust our own frailty; and though we may have too much reason to dread the Justice of the Almighty, nevertheless, if the wretched sinner humbles himself before his Maker, and calls upon him for help, God will not despise the sincere and contrite heart.

It is not possible for those to love and serve God, who will not know their Maker, or own his laws. The generality of mankind content themselves with saying, they believe there is a God; but of what nature his Power is, or for what reasons they are to believe in it, they do not trouble themselves to inquire. In the worship which they pay to their Creator, they are satisfied with what is rather an assent to an established and public sentiment, than a firm and settled conviction of his Divinity. Through fear, or indifference, they will not examine his Attributes; and continually led away by their passions, towards worldly objects, they know not God, they think not of him, but as something wonderful, mysterious, and far removed from them. They flatter themselves, that their actions are beneath the notice of such an awful Being; and therefore they willingly shake off all fear of ever being accountable for them. Or, if they suppose themselves present to his view, they regard him as a powerful and severe Master, whose slaves they are, who demands from them the perpetual sacrifice of every passion, and from whose terrible judgment they would hide their heads. They dread him as an angry Judge, but do not love him as a beneficent and merciful Father. Miserable and mistaken sinners!... who do not know that God is Love, and that those who do not love God, cannot know him; for to know and to love him, are one and the same thing.

O Lord God Almighty!...awful as thou art, and yet so easy to be approached, who sittest so high above this earth, and yet makest thyself lowly to thy poor sinful creatures; boundless in Power, above the universe, and yet preserving it with thy constant care—so just and terrible in thy wrath, yet so gracious and merciful to all who sincerely turn to Thee! How long shall weak and erring mortals forget Thee! And how can I, a wretched sinner, speak thy praise! –Oh! ...for a prophet's tongue, to awaken this hardened and insensible generation; and to call my fellow-creatures to repentance and salvation! —If I warn them to turn to Thee, O Lord, and to seek Thee in their own hearts, they know not what I say; for, to vain and profligate men, their own hearts are a mystery; a sad mystery of guilt and horror, on which they dare not turn their eyes; the examination of which they dare not attempt, and on which their reflections never rest. To fly from their own accusing hearts, they plunge into the ambition, the crimes, and the vain amusements of this world. To such were addressed those words of our blessed Lord, "If I have told you of earthly things, and ye believe not, how shall ye believe if I tell you of heavenly things?" Miserable sinners! They dare not look into their own hearts; how shall they be able to look upon God? Let me behold thy works, O Lord, for all else is but vanity and vexation of spirit!—Let me, through Jesus, they beloved Son, have my part in Thee, and in that blessed inheritance which passeth not away. O, wretched world! The light shines in darkness, and the darkness comprehends it not. He who knows not God, passeth his days in a lethargic dream, ignorant of the high design of his creation, and more miserable than if he had never existed: for, better were it never to exist, than without Thee, O Lord God Almighty!—Awake!—Arise, O man! Know thy great end; assert thy glorious privileges, and aspire to immortality—immortality of joy and happiness; trample under thy feet the pleasures of this sublunary scene, as far as they are at variance with thy high destination; call to mind, continually, that the great, the terrible day of the Lord will come, when the stars of heaven shall fall, and the powers of heaven shall be shaken; —when the astonished earth shall behold the Son of man, the Redeemer of mankind, coming in the clouds of heaven, with power and great glory, to judge the world, and to reward or punish its inhabitants forever. Tremble at the thought of these dreadful words, "Depart from me, ye cursed, into everlasting fire, prepared for the devil and his angels." Tremble at the fate of the unprofitable servant, who will be cast into outer darkness, where shall be weeping and gnashing of teeth; whose anguish and torments shall endure forever, in that fire which shall not be quenched. Oh! Remember, blind and insensate mortal, that thou canst not escape from death; and that our Savior's lips have told us, "after death, the judgment!" Remember that the Son of God hath said, "Heaven and earth shall pass away, but my words shall not pass away," till every tittle of them be fulfilled. Nor let us imagine that the serious consideration of this awful and terrible scene may be put off, till years or sickness more plainly show us the grave. How can we say that we shall live till tomorrow, or even till the next hour? Let us remember, that our blessed Lord hath declared, that this great and terrible day shall come as a thief in the night, and as a snare shall it be to all them who dwell on the face of the earth; and that "of that day and hour knoweth no man, not even the angels of heaven, but God only."

Let us, then, awake to conviction, and to the knowledge of our God, that we may, in that hour, be found "among those who believe, to the saving of our souls."

CHAPTER 4.
ON PRAYER, AND THE HOLY SACRAMENT

The excellency of Prayer consists neither in a set form, nor in a multitude of words; for God knoweth what things we have need of, and understandeth our thoughts before they are uttered, or even conceived by us. Prayer is an acknowledgment of our dependence upon God; it is also an act of desire: therefore Prayer must come from the heart; for with this only we can desire. But, to be acceptable to God, our prayers must be offered up for such things as we are sure he will approve of. Without this qualification, were we to pass the whole day in repeating prayers, or in reciting pious sentiments, they can avail us nothing. Our blessed Lord meant this, when he said of such worshippers, "This people draweth nigh unto me with their mouth, and honoreth me with their lips, but their heart is far from me." How few, alas, pray to God as they ought; for how few desire and pray for what is necessary to their salvation! The sacrifice of ourselves, the humiliation and conquest of our self-love, the entire submission o four will to God—these are the things for which, as Christians, we ought to pray. How many, full of themselves and of their own imaginary devotion and piety, have never uttered on true Prayer! Our Lord tells us, that the poor Publican, who lifted up his heart to God, with only the words, "God be merciful to me a sinner," was accepted before the Pharisee, who pleaded his own merits, and his long prayers, and whose self-love prompted him to despise the poor sinner who stood beside him.

When our hearts are sincerely filled with the love of God, our prayers are offered up to him, not merely through our self-interest in the things for which we pray, but with a fervent desire that we may pray for such things as it may please him to grant. We know not what is best for us, and frequently ask for what would prove our greatest misfortune; whereas, when we pray for grace to love and serve our Creator; when we "ask first the kingdom of God, and his righteousness," we have the assurance of our blessed Lord himself, that all other things shall be added unto us.

On this principle, Prayer becomes a duty easy to be performed at all times, and in all circumstances; for if we are unable to bow our knees before God, yet we can at all times bow down our hearts in his sight; and from our hearts the love of God can always ascend to him, without the aid of our lips. This is what St. Paul means, when he desires us to "pray without ceasing." God will ever listen to the desire of a heart, truly and humbly devoted to Him. He will ever hear the pious supplication of the poor in spirit; of those who are low in their own sight, and who feel their own vileness. The grace of God is ready to help all such, and "the Spirit of God itself maketh intercession for them, with groanings which cannot be uttered."

This state of the heart is therefore the very essence of Prayer; and though the occupations of the world, and our stations and business in it, may cause frequent wanderings of our thoughts from God, yet if we keep his grace alive in our hearts, we can never be separated from his love and care: it will be to our souls as a shining lamp, burning continually before the throne of God; and our Savior tells us, that "blessed are they, whom the Lord, when he cometh, shall find watching."

In order to keep up, and preserve in our weak and sinful natures, this state of mind, this blessed reliance on God, and (if we may so call it) responsibility to Him, two things are necessary to be observed by us: —First, that we carefully nourish and cherish it; next, that we avoid everything which may tend to weaken or destroy it. In order, therefore to keep alive the grace of God in our hearts, we should strictly, and every day of our lives, observe state hours of Prayer. To this should be added a moderate portion of religious reading and meditation on the Divine Nature of our Creator, and on his mercies to ourselves, with a constant habit of self-examination. These exercises should prepare us for the Holy Communion, which we should receive as often as we can. We should carefully avoid everything that can remove us from God, and sacrifice every attachment to such objects as may be displeasing to him. We should with doubt and fear shun every temptation of this king; especially profane and dissipate company, and the participation of any pleasures and amusements, which interest the passions too highly; in short, whatever may lead our hearts to forget God, or abate our zeal for his service.

Our religious reading should be confined chiefly to such books as will instruct us in the performance of our duties, and place us on our guard against our faults, particularly those which we are most liable to fall into from our passions, or our situation in the world.—Books of this sort will show us the greatness of God, and the wonders of his works, and teach us, at the same time what we owe to Him, and how infinitely we fall short of that obedience which is his due.

The duty of Prayer is to be regulated by situation and opportunity, and by the disposition and necessities of each person. But daily Prayer to God should never be neglected, except on the most urgent occasions. Meditation is also of the greatest use, in our way to salvation, on the wonderful works of God in the creation, and his infinite mercies in the redemption of mankind.

The laws and precepts of the Gospel can never be too deeply or too frequently considered by us; we should reflect upon, and examine them, till they become so habitual to our minds, as to be imperceptibly the rules and springs of our conduct, and the only light and guide of our souls. When the Divine Grace is thus cherished and strengthened in our hearts to the utmost of our power, its sacred light operates at once upon our conduct, and directs us in the way in which we should go; and this it does with a force and steadiness, which no longer require us to examine into its source: nor does it allow us to doubt its truth, any more than to question the reality of the sun's existence, when we behold that glorious luminary arising, to dispense to us the blessings of light and heat.

Our method of Prayer should be directed by our own reason and experience. Those who find an exact form of words most capable of confining the attention, and raising the soul to God, should always make us of it. Those who find their devotion restrained by adhering to one settled form of Prayer, are not commanded to do so; they are both at liberty to address their heavenly Father in what terms they choose. Let both parties take care that their Prayers be such as are proper to be made to the

Almighty, and that they are made with their hearts; they may then rest assured that God will graciously receive them.

The grade of God is particularly promised to the observance of that last and divine command of our blessed Lord, that we should receive the Holy Sacrament, which he has left us as a pledge of his love, as a remembrance of his most precious death, and as a means whereby, through faith, we become partakers in all the benefits of it. If we receive this Holy Sacrament worthily, with a true repentance for our sins; with love and charity to our fellow-creatures, and with a lively faith in the mercy of God, and the merits of our Redeemer, it will afford inexpressible comfort to our souls: But should we presume to approach our Lord's table unworthily, that is, without a strong faith in the Gospel, and without a strict examination of our own hearts, we should increase our danger, instead of enlivening the hope of our future salvation.

Too many good people are, however, deterred from receiving this most strengthening and refreshing food of their souls, by scrupulously fearing that, after all the preparation they can make, they are still unworthy to come. Thus they deprive themselves of the greatest blessing on earth, the greatest comfort of their pilgrimage in this life, considering God rather as a severe Judge, than (as he truly is) a merciful Father. But those who thus feel, should remember, that, though none of us are worthy of being received at that sacred table, yet we are all commanded to come: and hence we may hope, that by humbly attending, we may each time become less unworthy. And surely, after we have endeavored to prepare ourselves, to the best of our knowledge and ability, we may go without fear, and in time we shall find all our scruples and unwillingness vanish; and it will become not only an act of obedience to our God, but of so much comfort and happiness to ourselves, that we shall account it the greatest pleasure we are capable of enjoying in this world. By distrusting God's mercy, by giving admittance to these scruples in our hearts, and thus fearing to come to Him, we become guilty of a great sin. Let us, then, at all times, thankfully receive the Holy Sacrament; and, as we must live with our fellow-creatures, let us do unto them as we would they should do unto us. Let us live with faith and humility, and we may then be satisfied that we are accepted in the sight of God; not offering to Him the constrained obedience of slaves, but the voluntary service of children, to an all-wise and all-merciful Father.

We are sometimes inclined to believe that our prayers are not accepted by God, if we do not feel a certain degree of pleasure arising from the performance of this duty; an enthusiasm of love towards the Divine Being arising in our souls. This is a wrong idea: Prayer is not a charm of the imagination, or a sweet delusion of the soul; neither does it always produce the perceptible emotions of the grace of God in our hearts: It is our bounden obedience to a divine command; it is our self-humiliation before our Maker, the deprecation of his wrath, and the imploring of his assistance against the temptations of sin. Let us, therefore, draw near with a pure heart, in full assurance of faith, making our petitions in the Name of our Lord Jesus Christ, and relying on his Merits alone for God's acceptance of them.

CHAPTER 5
ON GOD'S GRACE AND PRESENCE WITH US

How delightful is the reflection to a true Christian, that God is at all times present with us! It is his voice which is heard in the secret whispers of conscience to our souls, recalling us to goodness when we err, and promising us pardon, if we sin no more.

When we fulfill our duty, we feel his more immediate presence within us; He inspires us with the good which we do, and he approves of it when done through him. Are we compassionate and charitable to our fellow-creatures in distress? Do we pardon the injuries which we may have received, or do we seek occasions of returning good for evil?—It is from God alone that such actions proceed; and the same all-gracious Power, which prompts us to do good, will reward our performance of it a hundred-fold. We need not look for the Almighty in the center of the earth, or seek for his power beyond the grave: He is ever present, ever near, nor need we turn our eyes from ourselves to behold Him. We are (as the Psalmist says) fearfully and wonderfully made; and the most marvelous of the Creator's works is the human heart. O, that men would, therefore, praise the Lord for his goodness, and declare the wonders that he doeth for the children of men! There is no situation, no state of existence in this world, in which we may not be sure of the protection of Heaven, and the directing hand of God, if our conscience tells us that we faithfully endeavor to deserve it: Were we placed in a desert, inaccessible to men, and unknown to the world, God could support us there; even there He could bless us with peace and plenty.

We should not be discouraged, or dismayed, if we do not at all times feel the same good dispositions; let us not fear that God has withdrawn himself from us, or that we are become unworthy of his grace; the very fear itself is a proof of the contrary; for a state of sin is mostly one of security. God often makes trial of us in this manner, and by leaving us to the workings of our corrupt nature, shows us what we are without his assistance. When we are made thus to feel our own natural depravity, we become more able to estimate justly the grace of God, and his merciful love towards us; and if we bear this state with hope and patience, while it brings to our minds a deep sense of our infirmity, it will prove an inestimable benefit to our souls. The operations of God's Holy Spirit may be often checked in our hearts, by the corruption of our nature, and the agitations of sin, especially if we are of a lively temperament and disposition, which is the most easily led away by the temptations of the world: but if we regret our errors as soon as we perceive them; if we sincerely endeavor to retrace our steps; we shall not finally lose ourselves in the road to salvation, though we may sometimes wander from it; we may even in some degree turn these wanderings to our good, if we view them as additional causes for distrusting ourselves, and praying more fervently for the grace of God. Human nature is weak, and prone to error; we are ever transgressing our duties, or failing in the performance of them: but still, if our will is inviolate; if we yield to temptation only through infirmity, and hasten to repent of our fault, and repair it as soon as we are sensible of it, we are yet in the favor of God, and may depend on his love. When we are most humbled by the sense of our own guilt, and ready to fear that God may cast us off forever, he is often most watchful over us, and most compassionate towards us. There is no trial so great to a virtuous mind, as this state of spiritual darkness, this sense of guilt, and longing for mercy and pardon from our offended God. This was the last trial of our blessed Savior—God withdrew himself from him; deprived him of the inward support and consolation of his divine presence, and abandoned him on the Cross, in that dreadful situation, to all the agony of his human nature. Jesus endured the sense of his heavenly Father's displeasure, and his soul was sorrowful and dismayed: and as he has known this state of spiritual suffering, his mercy and pity are ever ready to intercede with God, for all those who are sincerely sorrowful for their sins.

There are many voluntary faults, into which we constantly and daily fall, and yet we do not commit them with an *intention* of offending God. In the commerce of the world, our friends often reproach us with errors towards them. Of these, indeed, they had not expressly forewarned us; yet we knew our friends well enough, to be sure of their disapprobation of our conduct. Our state is the same, with respect to the grace of God in our souls: Our faults are voluntary; because though we do not commit them with reflection, yet it is with a kind of liberty, against a certain interior emotion of our conscience, which should make us hesitate, and suspend the action, until we have fully examined it. This, however, we seldom do; yet these are the calls for watchfulness, to which good minds should strictly attend: For we seldom see those who have the fear of God before their eyes, become guilty of great or crying sins; but as we improve in the love of God, we look on what we formerly accounted venial trespasses, as inexcusable and sinful errors; and so in fact they become; for the greater our knowledge of our duty, the greater is the crime of forsaking it. As by the light of the sun we perceive objects, which the obscurity of night concealed from us; so, when the grace of God shines more abundantly upon our souls, we discover a multitude of imperfections, till then unknown; a thousand black and malignant spots in our hearts, of which we had not suspected the existence. But if we really love our duty, this experience, instead of discouraging us, or causing us to neglect it, will incite us the more powerfully to tear down the edifice of pride and self-love in our hearts, and in its place to erect the Temple of God. There is no surer way of judging of our spiritual progress, than this acquaintance with our own turpitude, without being discouraged by it.

On all occasions, where we have the slightest suspicion of being wrong, the safe rule is to abstain; or, if the sense of wrong does not arise till after our commission of the fault, let us (as soon as our hearts are struck with it) at once, with humility, confess our error, patiently bear the blame of our fellow-creatures, and whatever mortification or shame our self-love inflicts on us, without seeking to extenuate our conduct, by any apology or excuse. And in the sight of God, oet us seriously deplore our infirmity, and with earnest supplication entreat from Him pardon, and an increase of those graces of which we have need.

The workings of divine grace in our hearts, are ever at war with our sinful passions, and cannot fail (without a miraculous operation of the Holy Spirit) to cause us much inward suffering: But it is not more the will of God, to work miracles every day, by his Holy Spirit, than by affecting the course of nature. It would be as great a miracle of grace, if a person devoted to the world were made to renounce at once its vanities, and appear dead to his interest, and to self-love, as it would be of nature, if a human being who went to bed a child, should rise up the next morning a full grown man. God does not permit the full operation of his divine grace upon our hearts at once, but he leads us on, by slow degrees, to as much perfection as we are able to attain; and trials and sufferings are the probationary exercises of our souls, which fit them for immortality.

The true end of religion is contained in that divine command, which God himself gave to Abraham,—"Walk before me, and be thou perfect." The presence of God with us, calms our minds, gives rest and peace to our spirits, during all the labors, trials, and sorrows of the day, and tranquil sleep to our bodies. When we have found God, we must endeavor to make our hearts a fit dwelling for him, by submitting and sacrificing to him (should he require it) everything most dear to us in this world; and by surrendering all to his holy will and pleasure.

If we were capable of giving ourselves up entirely to God, and of following continually the workings of his divine grace, we should not have much trouble in arriving at perfection; but, because we are by nature weak, and prone to error, because we are in this life in bondage to sin, and we have perpetually a will in our members, striving against the grace of God in our hearts, we too often fall back; yet, even so, we should not be discouraged. Let us, with all the strength which we have, confide in our God, and he will never forsake us.

CHAPTER 6
ON AFFECTIONS, AND RESIGNATION TO THE
WILL OF GOD

Those trials which come from God, are never without benefit to us, when we receive them worthily; since there is always a rich harvest of spiritual blessings for the afflicted religious heart. If human nature at first shrinks from sorrow, faith and Christian hop soon come to its support; the trial then appears easy to be borne: Receive it as from God, and its bitterness is past. In his own good time he will send his consolations; not those of the vain world, but such as shall speak comfort to your soul, strengthen your hope in Him, and confirm your submission to his decrees. Indeed, the peace which is always found in this submission is itself a great blessing, even without any exterior alleviation of sorrow. It is a peace so much the more pure, as it is unconnected with the world.

You may, therefore, bring your mind to such a Christian state, as to rejoice that it pleases God to visit you for your sins, by trials and sufferings in this world, instead of permitting you, by uninterrupted prosperity, to enter upon eternity with a hardened heart, and an unawakened conscience. As sinners, how grateful should we be to our Creator, that the short pains of mortality are thus mercifully substituted for the eternal pains of hell; that the society of the damned, and the torments of devils, are exchanged for a few years of worldly sorrow, under which we have the supporting hand of God, and by which we learn to grow in grace, and in fitness for his heavenly kingdom!

When calamity visits you, or misfortune threatens the remainder of your days, say not to yourself, Wherefore should I endeavor to support this, when I can perceive no prospect of relief, no hope of better times?—But how can you say this, when futurity is hidden from you?—Do you know what unforeseen events may change the gloom around you? Dare not, therefore, to invade the Attributes of God, in saying what *shall* be: support the present as he has commanded you, rely on his power, and trust in his mercy; believe in Him, and be at peace.

Our blessed Lord himself tells us, that sufficient unto the day is the evil thereof: God deals out our present trials to us as it seems best to himself. What are we, that we should dare to ask him, why is this laid on me? St. Paul tells us, that He is the Lord; 'let him do what seemeth him good." Whether he exalts or abases his poor sinful creatures, whether he wounds or heals their hearts, whether he appoints them life or death, he is still the Lord, and we are in his hands as clay, under the hands of the potter, to be molded and fashioned according to his will.

When God imposes a sacrifice upon us, or takes from us some beloved object, he does not leave us to endure the stroke unsustained; but if through the veil of sorrow which he spreads over us, we look up to Him, we shall, by the means of our mortal trials, reap everlasting joys. We are not to inquire of God, why he appoints us such trials, when we behold others exempt from them. Can we say how long our hitherto more fortunate fellow-creatures may continue untried with the like calamities?—It may be, that God sees we have most need of them: If we are faithful in what we understand, how limited soever our imperfect view may be of God's dealing with us, we shall find rest unto our souls, until it please God to dissolve our earthly tabernacle. We know, that then we shall have a building of God, a house not made with hands, eternal in the heavens. Let us, therefore, follow continually that guiding star, which beams upon our darkened way. Let us, with a willing and steady mind, embrace the occasions which each day may offer us of advancing towards our heavenly country, where we shall find our everlasting home. This is our daily bread, our manna in the wilderness of life: with this let us be content. If we presumptuously seek to look into futurity, our endeavors will be like the forbidden provision of the Israelites, not only superfluous, but noxious to ourselves.

It is the dependence of a child upon its parent, which God requires from us. He is our heavenly Father, and he dispenses to us our trials, as a parent appoints a task to his children. He does not overwhelm us with too much burden at once: He waits till we have finished one, before he lays another upon us. When God loves us, he does not leave our souls long in the temptation of prosperity; when we have passed through one trial, we are called to another; but his infinite mercy conceals from us the approaching blow, till we have regained strength to support it: And in thus receiving our daily allotments from God, we find continual reason for reproving our own sinful hearts; God then discovers to us our iniquities, which the mist of our self-love concealed. Occasion calls them forth, and we are filled with horror at perceiving them. We have, each of us, in the bottom of our hearts, a sink of infirmity and sin, which we cannot bear to own even to ourselves; we hate to cast our eyes inwards, upon what must give us so much mortification: yet there it lies; and if we refuse to look into our hearts, when God (by various means) calls upon us to do so, he then withdraws from us his grace, of which we are become unworthy; and by leaving us to continual prosperity, he abandons our souls to a state of blindness and security, which leads us to forget him entirely, until that awful hour overtakes us, in which we must appear before his Almighty throne, to give in our final account. How shall we, then, endure his anger? Will the prosperity and worldly enjoyments of our past lives then avail us? Or will they afford us even a drop of water, when, with Dives, we are tormented in that flame, where the worm dieth not, and where the fire is not quenched?

It is our duty to accept whatever God thinks fit to send us, notwithstanding our natural repugnance to it; we must receive it as coming from him, for an exercise of our faith, and a test of our allegiance to our heavenly King. If it pleases him to spare us any great and severe trials, it is well for us; and we need not torment ourselves with fearing that God is therefore the less watchful over us, or with imagining how we should have acted under them. When we are exempt from worldly sorrows and afflictions, let us humbly and gratefully offer up our thanks to God; and when they come upon us, let us patiently and submissively receive them, as becomes the disciples of Jesus Christ. This frame of mind, once established in us, will endure as long as we live, because it will be constantly nourished by the divine grace, provided we do not lose it by attachments to sinful objects, or unlawful pursuits.

God, indeed, often bestows great temporal blessings on wicked men, in order to show how little value he places on them. To those whom he loves, he sends afflictions and trials, that they may be hallowed and sanctified under his hand, and become more worthy of his love. Happy are we, then, when God visits us with trials and temptations (whether from within or from without) in this vain world. They are the sure marks of his love and care for our souls; and if we bear them as becomes his children, he will preserve us to everlasting life.

We are but too apt to accuse Providence when any great affliction falls upon us; we rebel against the will of heaven; forgetting that, by temporal calamities, God recalls us to himself. We should, then, pray to Him, not to deliver us from our sufferings; but (since it is his will that we should suffer) that he would be pleased to sanctify our afflictions to us, and give us patience and strength under them.—When the deep wounds of our hearts give us an abhorrence of the world; when they show us, too late, how deceitful are its dreams of felicity, and we turn from it, wretched and forlorn—at such a moment where shall we find rest, but in the mercy and goodness of God? The heart, suffering in its most delicate feelings, and disappointed in its most innocent, most virtuous inclinations, is driven back upon itself; but, no longer able to endure its own sensations, it flies to

God as its only refuge, and finds in Him a sure support, and an effectual consolation.

If we try to forget ourselves, and the world, all our misfortunes may be easily endured. It is a very wrong idea, that the devoting of ourselves to God cuts us off from the innocent enjoyment of this life, or that his service is hard; it is our own self-love that causes almost all our sorrows, since it is always at variance with the love of God. When, indeed, Providence tries us with any very sever deprivation; as the loss of a beloved child, or dear friend, God does not require us to be insensible to the blow, but to reflect that it comes from Him, and therefore must be for our good; that the beloved object which he has taken from us is far happier than before; and that, if we could lay aside our self-love, we should rejoice in his change. Our preparation for the joys of heaven, is through the calamities of this life, and our title to them is to be found in our manner of supporting those calamities. Our religion is but a vain form of words, and our piety nothing but imagination, if we do not patiently bow to the will of God. If we murmur against Providence, and in our afflictions seek for consolation from the world only, our hope is vain and our disappointment certain.

Let us not preach to others that which we fail to practice ourselves: When God tries us with great affliction, let us then call to mind the arguments which, in like circumstances, we have made use of to our fellow-sufferers. A soul devoted to God, and (as far as human frailty will permit) submissive to his will, may support the most dreadful calamities, and yet feel that peace, "which passeth knowledge." Suffering is the unavoidable lot of mortality; and to bear it in the easiest manner, must, therefore, be earnestly desired by us: But let us consider for a moment, how much better this case is to be obtained by those who trust in God, and believe in his holy Gospel, than by the unbelieving sinner. We can meet with no trials in this life, for which we may not find comfort and support in the Word of God. Nothing can so effectually disarm misfortune of its sting, as an acquaintance with the Gospel doctrines, a conviction of their truth, and the full assurance that everything which befalls us is directed by the unerring Will of God. This consideration will preserve our souls in peace, whatever be our lot in this world; and our sufferings will purify and prepare us for the unspeakable joys of the world to come. Happy are they who can thus suffer, and with calmness and tranquility apply to themselves those divine words of our merciful Savior,—"Blessed are they that mourn, for they shall be comforted: Blessed are ye when men shall revile you, and persecute you (if you bear it for my sake); rejoice and be exceeding glad, for great is your reward in heaven." St. Paul tells us, that God loves such as willingly and cheerfully give alms of their goods unto the poor. How much more will he, then, love those, who with faith and obedience resign themselves, their souls and bodies, a constant sacrifice to his Will?

We have often reason to acknowledge, that the most severe calamities have been sent for our good, though our frail nature cannot perceive this truth, while we are suffering under them. Those whom God loves he chastens, but he will never give them over unto death: His chastenings are those of a father unto his children; and if we receive them as we ought, they will advance us in the road to salvation.

St. Paul says, "I die daily." The good Christian may

be said to die daily, who bears the various sufferings of this life with his heart ever turned towards God, and with the example of our blessed Savior before him for his guide. If we believe in God, how can we question his power to replace to us, four-fold, even in this world, whatever we may have given up for his sake?—Was any one ever tried by the hand of God with greater calamities than Job; and what was his temper of mind under them? When urged to accuse his Creator, to curse God, and die; he replied, "The Lord gave, and the Lord hath taken away, blessed be the Name of the Lord." Let us remember this, and strive with the weakness and infirmity of our nature, that we may pass through our worldly sufferings, as gold through the furnace, more bright and valuable than before.

When it pleases God to send us any temporal suffering, or to afflict us, in our bodies, with any sore distemper, if we do not then humble ourselves before him, and thankfully acknowledge how infinitely short of our demerits are his chastenings, and how far the mercy of our Creator always exceeds his justice, we provoke his Holy Spirit against us; and with a mighty and stretched-out arm he afflicts us with greater calamities, in order to awaken our hardened souls to repentance and salvation: Therefore, when we mourn with inward sorrow, or smart under pain, let us bend our souls, and offer up our sufferings, before the mercy-seat of God; let us, with humility and confidence, think of his gracious promises to the penitent sinner; for God will not reject the prayer of the poor and destitute, nor despise the broken and contrite heart.

There are many trials in this life, which we are tempted to think are beyond our strength, and for which we are ready to arraign the Mercy of God; but we neither know the extent of his mercy, nor justly estimate our own strength: —What we call our weakness, is often only our laziness and irresolution; and it is our pride and self-love, which induce us to rebel against God, in the trials which he allots to us here.

To the unfortunate, the world is unfeeling, cold-hearted, and selfish; although those who are in sorrow or misfortune, have a peculiar claim to the pity and kindness of their more prosperous fellow-creatures. The Gospel tells us, that those whom God loves, he chastens; on this account, the afflicted and sorrowful should be also objects of love and compassion to those who truly love God. Any misfortune, which does not deprive us of our reason and our will, may, indeed, be most severely felt; but, however deep the wound, time will bring with it a most powerful consolation to all who believe in God, and trust in the merits of their blessed Redeemer. We suffer, but we are content to suffer, because it is the will of God. This perfect acquiescence in his Will, founded on the conviction of his Wisdom and Goodness, in all that he appoints for us, can alone disarm misfortune of its sting, and heal our deepest wounds.—Happy is that soul which places its hope and confidence in God, and with humility accepts from his hands both good and evil. How infinite is his goodness to us, miserable sinners!—What consolation does he pour into our hearts if, in the hour of affliction, we rest on *Him!* Our souls can be raised towards Him, without the help of speech, and the grace of his Holy Spirit can fill our hearts with comfort, and even "with joy unspeakable and full of glory." Let us, then, rest our wounded hearts upon our merciful God; and we shall be comforted, and enabled to endure whatever may be our lot, in this passing scene; remembering always, that it is *here*, where we must make good our claim to happiness *hereafter;* even to the happiness of eternity.

Have you lost, by death, an object in whom your heart was bound up; who was in the full enjoyment of lie, and its prosperity, and in whose society you hoped for many years of enjoyment? Oh!...consider (ere you accuse Providence for the stroke) that this death (apparently so untimely) is, possibly, the greatest instance towards you, both of the mercy and love of God. The creature so dear to you, may have been taken from some sad reverse of fortune, or from the commission of some great crime, which might have endangered his salvation: To secure this, therefore, God has removed him from temptation. The same loss is, perhaps, a call from God to yourself, and is intended to awaken you from that attachment which was binding you too fast to this world, and causing you to forget your Creator. Thus the stroke which, to secure his future happiness, takes him from the evil to come, detaches you from the world, and warns you to prepare for your own death, through that of one so dear to you. The pang of separation is, indeed, most bitter; our very vitals are lacerated with the wound; yet our merciful Father does not needlessly afflict his creatures: He wounds, only to heal the diseases of our souls. Let us, then, in the hour of calamity, hold fast by this conviction, and say, with Job, "Though he slay me, yet will I trust in him."—His mercy can be my support here, and my abundant recompense hereafter.

But what do we offer to God, in return for these instances of his love towards us; these awakening calls of his Holy Spirit?—How often do we turn his most precious gifts into so many means of showing our ingratitude for them! God is the source of our being, and of every enjoyment we can derive from it: The objects which we hold most dear, are only the vehicles of his goodness to us; yet they too often become the means of our ingratitude towards Him from whom they are sent. God is a jealous God; and when we thus force him to bereave us of what alienates our hearts from him, we should remember, that he chastens and corrects us, only that he may not give us over unto death.

O, just and righteous Lord God Almighty, myself and all belonging to me, are not mine, but *Thine* (though they may be dearer to my soul than life itself); give me grace to hold them as only lent to me during thy good pleasure; and fill my soul with that love for Thee, and that confidence in thy mercy, which thou requires. *Amen.*

We are ever expecting that God will bless us with prosperity, and we are not willing to see Him in sorrow and misfortune: —But what right have we to prescribe unto God? We must leave it to his wisdom, to appoint to us whatsoever pleases him. How often do we find reason to acknowledge the mercy and goodness of God to us, in that which we have at first accounted our greatest misfortune? God loves us most when he humbles and chastens us. Is it on God, or on the blessings and comforts which he bestows, that we place our love?—If we love God for himself alone, we shall soon be consoled for the loss of those blessings which he may reclaim, or those comforts which he may withhold from us, by the reflection that his love and presence are with us. The true love of God produces in us an entire submission to his will, and an entire acquiescence in all his dispensations.

In proportion to the rarity and excellence of the gifts of God to us in this life, is the duty which he requires of us, and the watchfulness which is necessary against an excessive attachment to them. When, therefore, we behold extraordinary beauty, talents, or moral excellence, in the objects of our love, we should endeavor not to forget the hour when we must be deprived of them, and which may be even now at hand. We should remember that they are not our own, but God's, and that they were but lent to us for a time. We found them, indeed, delightful, and they formed our happiness; but they belonged to God, and we have no right to rebel against him, when he has thought fit to reclaim them. The more precious his favors are, the greater is the risk which we run in possessing them. God loves us too well to abandon us to the snare into which he sees us ready to fall.—He recalls the temptation (to our mortal anguish, indeed); but (if it be not our own fault) to our immortal felicity.

Notwithstanding all our efforts, we find that so long as we are in the flesh, we must partake of its weakness.— This is our infirmity, and we must not be discouraged by it, for God does not ask of us more than we are able to give him. Our piety may be exemplary, and our inclinations to goodness sincere, yet the ties of affection, friendship, and reputation, are interwoven with our mortal state, and are with difficulty resigned. Too plainly is this proved, on the loss of any beloved object: the ties which bind us to it are become interwoven with our existence, and Nature will have her rights in mourning for what is gone. Yet it is only in affliction that we can truly judge of our spiritual state with God; and such are the times that show whether our religion is more than a mere form of words.

When God breaks asunder these dear and tender ties, what are our sentiments, and the feelings of our souls?—Do we remember that the trial comes from Him? And do we on that account submit to it with humility and patience?—"If this mind be in us," we need not fear the displeasure of God against the indulgence of our most tender feelings; for he knows whereof we are made. He does not command us (in this world) to put off humanity, or to possess the perfection of Angels; it is enough, if we endeavor, though with uncertain steps, to follow the rays of that divine Light which shines upon us.

If in our persons, God has bestowed on us great and noble talents, or superior qualifications, either of body or mind, we are the more answerable, both to God and to ourselves, for the use which we make them. Far from being the occasions of pride or self-love, they should excite us to watchfulness and distrust of ourselves; for God regards us with a strict eye, and will require a faithful account from us. Indeed, the chastisements of God are often inflicted on us, for our abuse of such precious gifts; and it is in mercy he then afflicts us, to recall us to a sense of our dependence on Him.

It is possible for us to turn the most acute bodily sufferings into blessings, by our manner of receiving and supporting them. Stretched upon the bed of sickness, or smarting under severe pain, if our souls rest upon God with hope and resignation, we shall not only bear our sufferings with patience, but even with a satisfaction of min, in the conviction that they are sent to us by our merciful Creator for our benefit.

If we are sorrowing under a misfortune, of which this

world affords no alleviation, the death of those most dear to us, let us humbly offer to our God the beloved whom we have lost. And what (after all) have we lost?—the remaining days of a being, whom we indeed loved, but whose happiness we do not consider in our regret; who, perhaps, was not happy here, but who certainly must be much happier with God; and whom we *shall meet again*, not in this dark and sorrowful scene, but in the bright regions of eternal day, and partaking in the inexpressible happiness of eternity.

How can we neglect, or waste the short and precious moments of a life, on which depends the happiness or misery of eternity?—If God sends affliction, let us suffer humbly, and with an unrepining spirit. If we bring our minds to this state of acquiescence, we shall be happy, not only in spite of our worldly sorrows, but even through them.

If we really look forward to another life, let us, while in this life, bear our cross with Jesus Christ. We know not how short may be the time allowed us to prepare by our temporal sufferings for a blessed eternity. "Our light afflictions, which are but for a moment, are not worthy to be compared with the glory that shall be revealed in us," if we pass through them in submission to the will of God. Death will then be a welcome release to us; it will be our happy admission to the presence of our God, "who will wipe the tears for ever from our eyes; from whose sight sorrow and sighing flee away; in whose presence is the fullness of joy, and at whose right hand there are pleasures for evermore."

It is through sickness and sorrow that we best fit ourselves for death. This life (even to the prosperous) is frail and short and full of anxiety; why, then, should we hesitate to sacrifice early to God, what is only worthy of our contempt—a vexatious and unsatisfactory world?

We must learn (as St. Paul says) to rejoice in tribulation; not, indeed, with a joy arising from our senses, but with the joy of our *will*. Sinners cannot conceive this joy; for they must inwardly suffer, even amidst sensual gratifications. The voice of conscience will not always be silent, but will often speak in thunder to their dismayed souls, threatening them with everlasting torments. How different is this state from the meek submission, the patient hope, the peaceful calm of the virtuous! With what fear and caution should we, then, choose our path, and weigh well the difference between the service of God, and that of the devil! We must serve either the one of the other; and that not merely for this short life, but for all eternity.

CHAPTER 7.
FAMILIAR ADVICE, AND PIOUS INSTRUCTION

Why do you complain so much of the afflictions which you suffer? It is because you will not distinguish in them the hand of God; and your self-love hinders you from perceiving it. Renounce yourself, and God will not abandon you; place your trust in Him, and he will help you. He sends these afflictions to awaken your soul, and to recall you to the love and obedience which you owe to him. Our misfortune is, that we too readily give up all our thoughts and affections to the creature, instead of the Creator; and this soon leads us into great sin: God therefore prepares for us a course of events, through which he by degrees takes from us the objects of our excessive, and therefore sinful, affections; and thus (unless we willfully resist him) he recalls us to himself. This operation is painful to us, and causes great anguish; but God sees it necessary to our eternal salvation. Do you accuse the surgeon of cruelty, who (when your flesh is corrupted) must, of necessity, cut to the bone, in order to save your limb?—No; for you are sure that in like manner he would treat his only son.

Our gracious God never afflicts us but for our good. He has no pleasure in the miseries of his children, but he pierces to the bottom of our hearts, that he may heal the ulcer which is there. When deprived of what we value, we weep under his hand, as a child does after some hurtful instrument which, in kindness, is removed from its reach.—What we think we have lost, God has placed in safety for us, where it can do us no harm; and he will restore it to us, forever, if we make ourselves worthy of it.

You know that no event can take place, no trial or affliction can come upon you unknown to God; why will you not, then, confide in him? He has numbered the very hairs of your head; he has counted the sands of the sea, and not one of them can be lost without his knowledge. Our Savior says, that a sparrow cannot fall without his Providence—how much more shall he save you, O ye of little faith! What to your narrow view appears of such magnitude, is nothing in the sight of God; a little more or less of this life to his creatures, are differences of no account in respect to eternity.—Eternity! O, wonderful and sublime idea! Compared with it, what is this life; and what matters it whether this body of mine, this poor frail dust, this vase of clay, be broken a little sooner or later?

Oh, how short and deceitful are the views of man! You lament the untimely fate of those who are called away in the flower of their years, or in the height of their prosperity; but for what do you lament?—God has taken the favored one from a corrupt world, from the midst of iniquity, and from the temptations of the devil: What, then, has he lost? On the contrary, is not the change to him his exceeding gain? But you will say, the bitter loss is mine: yet, examine it a little; you have lost the poison of worldly felicity, the cause, perhaps, of that forgetfulness of God, into which you were falling. Confess, then, the mercy of God, in that stroke which has taken him from the evil to come; and is preparing you, through it, to work out your own salvation. O, how truly is God our tender and merciful Father, even when he appears to crush and overwhelm us, till we are ready to rebel against him!—O, folly and delusion of mortality! Life passes away as a torrent rolls on its course. Already the past is to us as a dream; the present, even while we enjoy it, is sliding from us; days, months, years press one: Yet a few moments, and all in this world will (to us) be at an end. Alas! The time which we now account so long and so heavy, will appear to have been too short, if we have to look back on it unimproved.

Whatever, therefore, be your sorrow, how great soever your trial, submit yourself courageously and humbly to God; it is true, your sufferings may be severe, but God knows them to be so, and sees that they are good for you. The world, perhaps, has smiled upon you, and prosperity has hardened your heart. Would you continue until the awful moment of your death in a state of illusion, luxury, and pride, devoted to the vain joys of a world at enmity with Jesus? This world, for which we risk our eternal happiness, is inconstant and deceitful: How often do we find ourselves exclaiming against its baseness and ingratitude? Yet we are not ashamed of our excessive attachment to its deluding pleasures, while we forsake our God, who would deliver us from its bondage. Will you not, then, perceive how much you are your own enemy, in resisting his calls; in submitting yourself to the yoke of sin, and the dominion of the devil?—O, my God, who beholdest our misery, have mercy upon us, and heal us! Give us grace to look unto Thee, and unto thy dear Son, our Lord Jesus Christ. Endue us with faith, and hope, and love, and Christian patience, that we may behold our blessed Savior expiring on the Cross for our sins, and remember that he suffered to purchase for us everlasting life. Oh, cleanse our hearts from their impurities, that with hope, and pious confidence, we may turn to Thee, our true and only God.

Let us patiently endure the many painful events which cross our path through this life, and, as it were, interpose themselves between our God and us; let us take them as they come, and make use of them as so many steps towards heaven; remembering, that the evils which we are most inclined to murmur at, are those which may be most essential to our salvation. It is well for us, when we are thrown down, and cast to the earth, as St. Paul was at the gates of Damascus. We have need to be continually reminded that we have no help in ourselves, and that our only help is from God. Happy are we when we can endure our trials in silence, with a humble mind, yet with an invincible courage.—Patient in hope; strong only in God; and deriving support and consolation from Him alone. When we are tempted to repine, let us recall to our minds the image of our blessed Savior dying on the Cross—dying for those who placed him there. Remember his meek acceptance of that bitter cup, because it was sent him by his heavenly Father; and say, with Him, —"My God, not my will, but Thine be done."

You complain of your too great sensibility to the sorrows and trials of this life. You say that others are not so much to be pitied, because you think that few of them feel so acutely as you do; but of that you cannot be certain; and were it the case, still you are not to make it a cause of complaint against your Creator, that he has given you this deep sensibility, nor to suppose that he will require the less patience from you on that account. You are to look upon this part of your character as an additional trial, and to remember that you must answer to your Maker for this, as well as every other quality, according as you use or abuse it.

We know that, "in this world we must have tribulation;" we ought also to know, and to remember, that we deserve it: Yet we are always surprised and discontented when trial comes upon us, as if it were both undeserved and unnecessary for us. It belongs only to those who are perfect in the love of God, to receive trials with *joy*; but the mercy of God has regard to our weakness, and he is satisfied with our resignation and submission. It is true, that we must feel for ourselves, but it must be with an entire submission to the Will and unerring Wisdom of the Almighty. And how great is the consolation which this reflection ought to afford us!—for upon unerring Wisdom we may surely rest, even while its severity appears extreme to us. Thus we may become strong in our own weakness, by resting all our burthen upon God. St. Paul says, "I take pleasure in infirmities, in reproaches, in persecutions, in distresses, for Christ's sake—for, when I am weak, then am I strong" in Him.

God has condescended to call himself a faithful and a just God towards his creatures: Let us not doubt this gracious declaration, and when he afflicts us, let us not despond: Let us trust in Him, for he knoweth whereof we are made, and he will pardon our weakness, if we exert ourselves to the utmost of our power. We are told by himself, that "those whom he loves he chastens;" and when he appears to have overwhelmed and forsaken us, he pities our infirmities, and proportions our trials to our strength. The sufferings which, when at a distance, we have supposed ourselves unable to bear, will, on their near approach, be found not insupportable. Our imagination always magnifies calamity, and our self-love is ever increasing our sufferings. But every man's life is equally in the hands of God, and all the events of it are appointed by him.—To one he gives life—to another death.—"Let him do what seemeth good to Him, for he is the Lord."

This subject further treated under the following title of ABSOLUTE RESIGNATION.

CHAPTER 8
ABSOLUTE RESIGNATION

There are few precepts more strongly enforced in the Gospel, than that of conforming ourselves to the will of God, and the example of Jesus Christ, who, we are told, was in all things submissive to his heavenly Father. All virtue consists in our will and intentions, and the regulation of them according to the influence of divine grace. Our Savior means this when he told his disciples, "the kingdom of God is within you." We need not possess great talents, or perform brilliant actions in this life, to secure the happiness of the life to come: to love God, and to obey Him, is sufficient to ensure our everlasting felicity. Different situations and emergencies call for the practice of different virtues; but a pure intention of mind is equally applicable to all occasions, and all times. To desire, then, for ourselves, nothing but that which God pleases to send us, and to submit ourselves in all events to God, is indeed to have the kingdom of God within us; for thus we fulfill the petition of that divine prayer which is taught us by our blessed Lord—"Thy will be done on earth as it is in heaven;"

leave, therefore, to your gracious God, all your cares, and all your desires. It is not just that you should use your will against your Maker, to whom you belong. God has endued you with free will, only that it may be your own choice to give up that will to him; and that if you counteract his beneficent intentions towards you, you may be without excuse for so doing.

A mere desire to obey the laws of God, without unconditional and unreserved submission, is not the service, which God requires of us. Establish, therefore, this one truth in your mind, and let it not be in the power of any worldly occurrence to shake it—that there is nothing of such essential consequence to your happiness here, and hereafter, as this unconditional submission, and meek surrender of yourself, to the disposal of God. Our Savior's gentle rebuke to Martha is here very applicable, when she complained to him that her sister Mary had left all her domestic occupations to attend to the instructions which our blessed Lord was delivering to those about him; —"Martha, Martha, (said he,) thou art careful and troubled about many things, but one thing is needful."— We are not, however, to understand these divine words in too literal a sense, or to suppose that Christ condemned or forbade all concern for the things of this world; for as long as we remain in this life, we cannot prosper, nor even exist, without some care for the body; but we must learn to submit, at all times, the event of all our endeavors and undertakings, of every kind, to our merciful Father, and receive whatever issue he may appoint to them, with acquiescence in it, holding fast our obedience and submission to his will, as the one thing needful. Until you have attained this frame of mind, you will be always a slave to the reverses of life, dissatisfied with yourself and others, and full of suspicion and reserve in your commerce with the world. Your good intentions will avail you but little, and your piety (however sincere) will only reproach and torment you, unless God is the rock of your confidence, and the resting-place of your hopes. If you will but indulge the virtuous inclinations with which God inspires you, you will resign yourself entirely to the guidance of Him, who has loved you so tenderly, that he has given his only Son to die for you. Indeed, God's love towards you is a thousand times more tender than that of your earthly parents: he follows you everywhere, even while you stray far from him. As the good shepherd seeks his wandering flock, he seeks and invites you to his fold again. Nay, even while you persist in wandering, he does not leave you; he renews his gracious call, and rejoices when you will hear it. Shall we then refuse to hearken to this voice of mercy, which offers consolation to all our sorrows, and pardon to all our sins, and says to us (if we will but return to him), "Go in peace, and sin no more."

Let us but make ourselves indifferent to the world and its allurements, and our resignation to the will of God will become easy to us. When we can bring our minds to receive good and evil at the hand of God, with the same spirit of humble thankfulness, and trust in him, we may hope that we are in the right path. We are today prosperous and happy, let us be thankful for our blessings, and enjoy them with moderation; tomorrow is hidden from us, and God will order it according to his good pleasure. To every man is appointed his daily bread; sometimes, indeed, it is unpalatable, and bitter to the taste, but we have no right to refuse it from the hand of our Creator.

Men desire a life of enjoyment and gratification, but we are told in the Gospel, by our Savior himself, "that those who endure unto the end shall be saved." If, therefore, we desire to be saved, to enter into the eternal joys of heaven, and to stand in the presence of God, we must prefer the Cross of Christ, with all its humiliations, to the seducing pleasures of the world; and we must abide in this preference, not only with patience, but with cheerfulness. And, in fulfilling our duty, surely we have more cause for joy, than is to be found in the vain, or the sinful enjoyments of this life. So long as we follow the right path, we need not fear, for the blessing of God is with us, and the promises of salvation are before us, while sinners have nothing to hope for beyond the present moment. Patience, therefore, is no less our interest than it is our duty: we must be patient in all things; patient with our sufferings, patient with our remedies; patient with others, and patient with ourselves: we must neither indulge our infirmities, nor be discouraged by them; but we must watch over ourselves continually, and implore the Father of Mercy to counteract, by his divine grace, the evil tendencies of our souls. Submit yourself, therefore, to the will of God in every situation; and if anything in it appears to you cruel and unnecessary, remember that you are not a competent judge. Grief too often dwells in the imagination alone, and the most severe trials are often much less when they are felt, than while they were apprehended.

St. Paul tells the Philippians, that "unto them it was given, not only to believe in Christ, but also to suffer for his sake." All men should apply these words to themselves, when trials and afflictions come upon them; for to those who truly love God, these are no less marks of his favor, than the things which are usually accounted blessings. Wherefore should we receive good at the hand of God, and not evil also? And wherefore should we receive evil from him with murmuring or rebellion? In this way the devils endure the torments of hell; and shall we commence our eternal punishment on earth, by thus resembling them? But let us suppose our whole life to be almost one continual scene of suffering; we know that for those who endure with hope and patience, death will be a sure and blessed passport to everlasting happiness. To believe in the words of our Savior is not alone sufficient, for we are told by St. James, that "even the devils believe and tremble;" let us therefore neither suffer, nor believe as they do; let us suffer and believe like the true servants of Jesus Christ, looking forward to the rewards which he has set before us; humbling ourselves in his sight; confessing our own weakness; and beseeching him so to strengthen us, that whether in doing, or in suffering, we may perform his will.

Let us all strive to repeat, with a pure heart, those words of our blessed Savior, —"Father, I have finished the work which thou gave me to do." God has appointed to us all, in this world, a part to perform; and all our concern should be, to perform it well. In so doing we may hope to be included in the blessed call, with which the Lord of Glory will address his elect, on that great and final day, that shall forever determine the fate of mankind: "Come, ye blessed of my Father!" O, my God, give me grace to be faithful and active in doing thy will; my only part is to choose whatever thou has chosen for me, and to thine infinite mercy I resign myself. We are all unwilling to acknowledge the wisdom and goodness of God in the trials which he appoints to us.

We are apt to say to ourselves, If God loves us, why should he take pleasure in afflicting us? His power could prevent our sufferings, why then cannot God make us good, without rendering us miserable? God could, without doubt, allow us all to pass through this life free from sorrow or misfortune; for with the Almighty, nothing is impossible. The events of life, and the hearts of all men, are in his all-powerful hands; but it has not seemed meet to him to allow us to enter into his heavenly kingdom, without some portion of suffering in this world. God might also have ordained, that man should at once attain his full stature, and the maturity of his reason; but it has pleased our Maker to send us into this world, small, weak, and helpless, and to appoint us to attain, by slow degrees, the use of our faculties, and the development of our intellectual powers; we are not to ask, why is this so? It ought to be sufficient for us that God has willed it so. We must in silence adore his unerring wisdom, and submit. It is not required of us, neither is it possible for us, to comprehend all the wonderful ways of our Creator; but of this we may be sure, that we cannot be worthy of his favor, unless we resign ourselves wholly to his will, and walk according to the laws which he hath set before us.

God has commanded us to endeavor after perfection in his service. True Christian perfection is a state of as much happiness as this world admits of. It has no constraint, no severity, no languor; and the practice of it is as easy as it is delightful. God demands our heart. You must know and feel, that when your heart is truly engaged, you do not find anything too severe, which the object of its attachment may exact of you. Wherefore then will you fix your heart on the vain, sinful, and perishable things of this world, when God, the glorious, the merciful, the beneficent God, offers to us, in his heavenly kingdom, an eternal inheritance of joy unspeakable? When once you have made your duty to him your first object and care; when you have subdued your will, and conformed your desires to whatever he appoints for you, you must be happy; for *content,* and *peace of mind,* and *freedom of heart,* will be yours, in every situation. The true Children of God do not fear the trials and sorrows of this life; they know them to be but transitory, and that they shall be amply recompensed for them by their heavenly Father. They may endure many privations, and make many sacrifices, but their will is ever firm and tranquil; they endure all for God's sake; and to whatever he appoints for them in this world, their hearts, continually say, Amen.

God requires from us a heart which is not shared with any of his creatures; but which makes him our first and great object, and his glory and service our constant end and aim. When we have attained this disposition of soul, we may turn even the folly and vanity of the world to our good. Happy they who can thus give themselves unto God! They are unmoved by the envy, the baseness, and the ingratitude of men; by the instability of fortune, and the inconstancy of friends; by the artifices and the snares of enemies; they escape the misery of an ill-spent life, the cruel remorse attached to criminal pleasures, the horrors of a profane deathbed, and the fears of eternal damnation.

There can be no peace nor comfort for those who resist the will of God. The world, and all that it can offer, must be full of anguish and disquiet for those wretched sinners who are at enmity with him. The only real joy to be found on earth, arises from the possession of a pure conscience towards our Creator. Oh, how preferable a state is the favor of God (even while we are oppressed by the misfortunes of this life), to the height of worldly prosperity without this divine rest, which frees us from the influence of our passions, refines our desires, and delivers our souls from the delusion of sin! O, blessed state on earth; when we may hope that we are in the favor of God! This enlarges our views, opens to us the bright prospect of immortal and unspeakable happiness, and enables us to disregard everything which would oppose our endeavors after it.

"They who sow in tears shall reap in joy." These are the consoling words which the Scripture has offered to us, and we are also assured by it, that the sufferings of the present time are not worthy to be compared with the glory which shall be revealed in us, if, by patient continuance in doing and suffering the will of God, we seek from his mercy a happy immortality. Then God himself shall wipe our tears away, and heal the deepest wounds that may have pierced our hearts in this life of trial.

One of the deepest wounds which our hearts can receive in this life, is caused by the death of those who are most dear to us.—It is a sorrow which admits of no other consolation, than that which is found in absolute submission to the Will of God. This, and this alone, may enable us at last to say, even while we mourn—"My Creator has laid his afflicting hand on me, and I was nearly crushed beneath the dreadful blow. Alas! I had almost forgotten my God. My irreparable loss had overpowered me, and my soul refused comfort; my conscience now reproaches me with rebellion against the decrees of heaven. Still, indeed, I mourn, and shall forever mourn, the object who was the delight of my existence; but I am become calm, and resigned to a trial, which I know has come from God. There is nothing certain in this world, except that we shall leave it. My beloved _____ has died the death of the righteous, and has exchanged this darkness for everlasting light. In piety and resignation, in faith and holy hope, he went to his Creator, and has (no doubt) received his bright reward. In taking him from me, God has preferred his happiness to mine. My wound is deep, and my heart is sad, and in this world nothing can make me any amends. But God requires me to submit to his will; and faith points out to me that bright abode, where he whom I have lost is now in everlasting bliss. O, my God, look down in mercy on me, and let me so offer up my sorrows, as to expiate my rebellion against thee!"

God has sent us into this world to make us worthy of his eternal kingdom, and by the patient endurance of our trials here, to exalt our happiness hereafter. Happy, therefore, are they who in this life assist in bearing the Cross of Christ. This doctrine is hard, and difficult for human nature to receive; but the faith of a Christian can accept it, and the love of God can enable him joyfully to take up his burthen, and to follow Jesus. Our blessed Lord himself has told us, that "those who endure unto the end, shall be saved." Let us, therefore, go on to "fight the good fight," that we may finish our course with joy, looking unto Jesus, the author and finisher of our faith, who has laid up for us a crown of righteousness. Amen.

Reliance on God is equally our duty, with that of absolute submission to his will. The Gospel tells us, that a steady faith in the promises of God, is necessary to our salvation; and our own reason must assure us, that without it we can have no claim to them. The promises of everlasting life are only to be obtained through faith; and for this we have the example of Abraham, who believed in God, when he had no visible prospect to encourage him. Behold, too, the blessed Virgin, the mother of Jesus! When the Angel of the Lord declared his divine message, and told her, that while she was y et a virgin, she should conceive and bear a son (by means the most miraculous), she doubted not, but exclaimed, "Behold the handmaid of the Lord, be it unto me according to thy word."

St. Paul addresses the Corinthians in these words, — "Be ye followers of me, even as I also am of Christ." He exhorts them to put away all hurtful compliance with the world, all sinful indulgence of their passions, and all remissness in godly works. This advice is addressed to Christians in general, as well as to the Corinthians, and therefore is equally applicable to the world at present. The practice of virtue does not consist in words; nor shall we ever by these alone enter into the kingdom of heaven. IN order to arrive at that blessed state, our life must be a continual warfare. We must strive for victory, and learn to obtain a complete dominion over all our evil inclinations, and a constant willingness to resign all we have to God's disposal. We must be content, in whatever situation he has placed us, awaiting his good pleasure for every blessing and enjoyment of our lives; relying solely upon God for all things; making use, indeed, of every lawful advantage for the success of our worldly affairs; but trusting for that success (with tranquility and confidence) in God's good pleasure; —thinking (not only without fear, but with gladness) that we are always in the presence of God; believing that God's mercy will pardon our sins; and through this belief, rejoicing in his presence and power over us. This is the true spirit of the Christian life; and in conforming to this, to the utmost of our power, we may so pass through the temptations and troubles of this world, that we may depart in peace when our hour is come.

Whilst you live without God in the world, you are the continual sport of fortune, and a prey to the injustice, the malignity, and the evil designs of men. Your unrestrained passions expose you to those of others, and your unbridled desires associate you in their crimes: Your pride and self-love (which are incompatible with those of your neighbor) foam and swell against opposition, like the billows of the angry ocean, and occasion you a thousand shipwrecks. You exist in constant warfare with all around you, and know not where to rest. Is this a state (even with worldly prosperity) to be preferred to the holy hope, the divine calm, the conscious trust in Providence, possessed by that soul, which having renounced its self-love, and restrained its passions, walks humbly with its God?—View the world as it now is, and as it has ever been, and you will find, that, according as forgetfulness of God and irreligion prevail, such has been, and such will ever be, the evil state of society. Behold all the children of Adam serving as instruments of punishment to each other!—See the one-half of mankind rendered miserable by the other, who equally oppress them in their turn!—Behold, in every nation, in every family, and even between two friends (not influenced by religion) the never-ceasing divisions caused by pride and self-love!

If you love and serve God, you are then independent of the world; its passions, its follies, and its crimes affect you not: You will then know (and it will be your supreme comfort) that the events of the world, and the wickedness of mankind, are under the control of Him who is all-powerful; that they cannot pass the bounds prescribed by Him; and that they are only permitted for his all-wise and inscrutable purposes. You will then have placed your treasure in heaven, where it will be secure. Though shame, and grief, and oppression, and death itself come upon you, you will hear the encouraging voice of your blessed Savior—"Fear not them who can hurt the body." How weak is their power!—Even when they take away our life, they can but shorten that term, which must soon of itself have ended. They can but at once give us death, which the chances of every day may occasion, and which the lingering torments of a sick-bed might have made much more painful. Remember that, in this life, you are to suffer, whenever it pleases God; and that our Savior has said, "Miserable are they, whose consolation is of this world." Those who seek for their happiness here, have no right to expect the joys of heaven. We shall one day know the spiritual advantage of our worldly trials; the anguish of them will then have passed away; but the glories of heaven, and our blessed reward there, will last to all eternity.

Put your trust in God, and rely on him without fear: Remember the words of our Savior to one of his disciples,—"Wherefore didst thou doubt?" Still, however, take care to preserve your humility, and let the experience of your own weakness make you doubt even your best resolutions, until you have implored the blessing of God on them. O, how deplorably weak and blind are we! And how merciful is our God! Put your whole confidence, therefore, in Him, and take refuge from your errors, by casting yourself and them at his feet.

Acknowledge how poor is that vain-glory, whose best resolutions are so unstable; God will then send you the grace of his Holy Spirit, and make you strong in *Him;* and, in time, you will reflect with astonishment that, at any time, you have placed your trust either in yourself, or in the world.

Seek not to penetrate into futurity, neither encourage a habit of anticipating good or evil. Our trials do no always come from those occasions which we may have foreseen. God frequently takes us by surprise, and sometimes, in those objects on which we most fondly rest our hearts, and in those moments in which we think ourselves most secure. The evils which we have imagined for ourselves, often vanish before the eye of reason, and it is not in our own power to choose where the blow shall fall. Let, then, the obedience of every day, and of every hour, be your daily bread: Live upon the will of your God: He provides for you celestial manna; be satisfied with it; it is not in your power to lay it up in store, or to say how much of it God will give you; all that you have to do, is to use it in such proportions as you receive it. Strive to pass your life in peace, simplicity, and resignation; place your hopes of happiness in God, and not in his creatures, and you will then be secure; for on him you may rely with full confidence.

We must sow in tears, in this world, if we expect to reap the joys of heaven. Those who are enslaved to the enjoyments of the present life, desire to reap before they have sowed; they wish that God should make the road smooth which leads to him, and are unwilling that his service should cost them any trouble.—Self-love induces them to wish for eternal happiness, yet withholds them from making any sacrifices to obtain it. But we are assured, that the sufferings of the present time are not worthy to be compared with our eternal reward; and the time will come, when the sinner will look back with horror and dismay on the vain and empty joys of this world, and on his own blindness, in preferring them to the happiness of that heavenly kingdom, where God himself will be the portion of the righteous forever.

The Gospel tells us, that "the Peace of God passeth all understanding;" and it is, indeed, to be estimated rightly, only by those who enjoy it: —Seek, therefore, to attain this peace; for, if you possess it, you will pass through the present life without solicitude, and you will regard the life to come without fear. Your state hereafter is, indeed, in the hands of God; he has instructed you how you are to prepare yourself for it: —If, therefore, you follow his commands, you may with confidence leave the rest to him. Each day brings with it a certain proportion of good and evil; it is in your power so to receive it, as to reap good to your soul, even from the evil; nor can you ever want occasions of renouncing yourself, and overcoming your passions. —Alas, you will never make use of half of those which you have; you may, however, believe, that no sincere desire of doing this, is lost in the sight of God: when, therefore, your weak nature fails, call with the more earnestness for his aid; and be assured that he will vouchsafe it to you.

CHAPTER 9
ON RETIREMENT FROM THE WORLD

Since Providence has appointed our place in society, and given us active duties to fulfill, we shall not do right if we desert our station. A soul devoted to God, and zealous for his service, will not feel the necessity of flying from the world, and seeking salvation in solitude and retirement. Undoubtedly, there have been good and pious men who have devoted themselves to God, through a seclusion from the world, and to whom he has shown peculiar marks of his favor; but we should consider how few these are, and how much more useful they might have been, had they devoted themselves to god in society, and sought for his favor in assisting and benefiting their fellow-creatures.

The frequency of our retirement from the world, of prayer to God, and attendance on the holy Sacrament, must partly be regulated by the demands on our time, which may arise from our necessary worldly employment; and where there is leisure and opportunity, we should do well to make much use of these great helps to our final destination. Religious retirement, however, should depend on our place and station in life, and upon the necessity of it to the welfare of our souls: for, if we have large families to provide for, or our own subsistence to gain, we please God more by fulfilling our active duties, than by retiring to our closets, to meditate upon our Creator. The sure way to please God is to do his will, and to serve him in any station to which he has called us, without murmuring or repining.

When you would lift up your mind to God, it is not always necessary to wait until you can enter into your chamber, and close your door, and fall upon your knees before him: This (on account of your daily occupations) may not be often in your power; you are not, however, to suppress the desire to do so, far less to imagine that your want of time is a sufficient excuse for not feeling that desire. The most secret offerings of the heart are known to, and will be accepted by, that God who seeth in secret; and the most hurried moments, and busiest scenes of your life, may be blessed and sanctified by Him, if your *heart* is sincerely, confidently, and humbly lifted up to Him. This is the Apostle's meaning, when he says, "Whether ye eat or drink, or whatsoever ye do, do all to the glory of God."

A day seldom passes, which does not afford us some opportunity of being useful to our friends, or of pardoning our enemies; of bearing with the infirmities of those about us, or of conferring benefits upon them: But a life of seclusion from the world (into which we are sent to prepare ourselves for a better, by the exercise of active virtues) must necessarily prevent the exercise of many benevolent dispositions.

CHAPTER 10
OF MELANCHOLY, AND SCRUPLE IN RELIGION

You complain of the unhappy state of your mind on religious subjects, and you do not look into the cause of it, nor apply the proper remedy. The cause is, that you cannot bear to wound your self-love, by the mortifying view of your own faults: But you can never enjoy peace of mind, till you have destroyed this pride of spirit, and acquired humility; till you can heartily detest all your sins, and confess them to God, without reserve.—You are listening, at present, to the voice of your passions, yet you find it impossible to stifle that of your conscience; and thus, you can neither fully enjoy the criminal pleasures to which you are inclined, noir can you feel any confidence in god, nor any delight in his service.—You must shut your ears to "the voice of the Charmer, charm he never so wisely." You must steadily resist the temptations of the world, and with humility look upon your own unworthiness. God does not require us to lacerate our flesh, or to torment our bodies, in order to show our devotion to Him. A humble and contrite heart, a meek and docile spirit, ready to do and to suffer anything in obedience to his Will, are the only acceptable offerings in his sight.

We are told in the Gospel, that at the day of judgment we shall be accountable for every idle word, as well as for every sinful action. This has been the cause of much scruple and disquiet to many good and religious people, who, misled by too literal an interpretation, have lived in constant self-reproach, though they have nothing to accuse themselves of in this respect, but the trifling and venial faults of conversation, in which they are guilty of no malignity, nor the least intention of injuring any one. Let those who are unhappy through this scruple, remember, that God is too just, too merciful, to punish them eternally for such errors. We may safely confide in his pity and long0suffering towards our infirmities, when he has given his only Son to redeem a sinful world.

The Scriptures tell us, that we are to mortify our desires and affections in the flesh; but we are not to understand this as a prohibition of every innocent and reasonable gratification. It is a false and absurd maxim, that we are always to make a choice of what mortifies us most; for in this sense, we should ruin both our heath, fortune, and reputation; we should be ever grieving our relations and friends, and we should fail in the performance of many good works, which Providence throws in our way. We are not, therefore, to understand this precept in too rigorous a sense, but as a prohibition of those enjoyments, which are either sinful in themselves, or which may be prejudicial to our health. We may become guilty in several ways, by the unrestrained indulgence even of lawful gratifications, and fail in that fortitude with which we are commanded to resist temptation; and if we fail in a small matter, how shall we acquit ourselves in a greater one?—We set a bad example to those who, perhaps, look up to us for a good one: by allowing the principle of rectitude in our minds to be invaded, though in a small degree, we prepare the way for a greater dereliction of it.

Many good and pious Christians are at times a prey to melancholy, which weakens the bodily constitution, and fills the heart with anguish: —For this, Providence offers us a remedy; and let us make use of it. While we are under the dominion of melancholy, we should avoid all difficult and painful business as much as we can; we should take care of our bodily health, and make allowance for the weakness of our minds.—We must seek for comfort from God by prayer, and we must strengthen our spirits by cheerful reading; taking special care, however, that it be not of a kind either to flatter our vanity, or our passions; we should seek the conversation of our most cheerful acquaintances; in short, we may make use of every lawful and reasonable method to overcome this melancholy, and recall a more lively and energetic temper of mind. Happy are you, if, in such a case, you have a good and sensible friend, to whom you can unburden your heart; this is the greatest of all consolations to a wounded and dejected spirit. Alas, I have too often felt that sorrow and dejection, when too long suppressed, prey with redoubled violence on the heart; whereas, when we impart our distress to a friend, we find, even in doing so, something that alleviates our pain, and seems to pour a balm into our wound.

If we are, nevertheless, still a prey to melancholy, we have sure help in God. Let us, with humble and earnest supplication, seek from Him that hope and comfort, which he alone can give; patiently enduring the continuance of such sensations, and accounting them (as they really are) a species of trial. Instead, therefore, of yielding to the languor of our minds (which may cause us to fail in our daily and positive duties), we should, with increased ardor, seek in those very duties the further means of cure; and let us also remember, that whatever infirmity of our nature is not sinfully encouraged, or weakly submitted to, is a further inducement to our gracious God to grant us the aid of his Holy Spirit. God sees the heart, and his judgment is unerring. He gives his assistance to all who sincerely struggle against their spiritual weakness; and when, through his aid, we have resisted any doubt, or overcome any temptation, we have more favor in his sight, than if the temptation had not assailed us—than if those terrors had never oppressed us with doubts of our spiritual state.

We must, therefore, constantly and unremittingly exert ourselves to fight our way through every obstacle towards our heavenly Canaan, still making these very obstacles so many greater incitements to a steady courage and unshaken faith. And let those who are subject to religious doubts and terrors of mind, yet who sincerely endeavor to perform their duty, remember, for their comfort, that this state of mind, however painful, is much more safe, and more acceptable to God, than confident security, and self-satisfaction, which is but the result of vanity. A soul which is penetrated with a deep sense of its own unworthiness, which, afflicted and sorrowful, even unto death, cries out with our blessed Lord on the Cross, "My God, my god, why has thou forsaken me?" is beheld by our heavenly Father with much more compassion, than the more confident soul, which trusts in its own merits; though the latter may have more of the forms of righteousness.

Our imagination is, however, too active, and apt to lead us after vain and seducing objects, which, for a time, will obscure, and, perhaps, overcome our best inclinations, and weaken our sense of duty. But despair not. If, when the delusion vanishes, and the Divine Grace touches your heart, you repent of your errors, and endeavor to regain the right way, God will not hastily separate himself from you; nor, when your heard is with him, will he too severely judge your infirmity. Let us but endeavor steadily to keep up in our souls a lively sense of God's continual presence, and we need not be too scrupulous or unhappy about our conduct; for we shall find this sense of God's presence with us the most effectual check upon our passions—but if ever this sense should seem to be lost amidst the multiplicity of our occupations, and the various occurrences of life, let us stop and examine ourselves, and if we find that (although we may have been too much engrossed by the world) God is really our first object, we may still hope to find ourselves in his favor; for he is a most merciful Father, and he ever beholds mankind with compassion and patience; nor, until they have repeatedly provoked him, does he give them up to their own sinful desires, or deny them the grace of his Holy Spirit.

There is a species of religious melancholy, which apparently proceeds from the excessive love of God (if we may be permitted to make use of such a term), but in reality originates in the love of ourselves. We wish to feel that assurance of God's grace being in us; we desire to think ourselves certain of his favor; yet we are not willing either to follow the Divine Laws, or to resign those objects of our pursuit, which entice us to sin. We desire God's favor, that we may feel at ease concerning our state in a future world; we cannot divest ourselves of the fear of God, nor the hopes of happiness hereafter, yet we cannot bring ourselves to give up the world and its sinful enjoyments. We are not blind to our faults; our pride is grieved and mortified at the knowledge of them, but we do not take the trouble of correcting them. We are, however, willing to mistake this uneasy sense of mortification, for repentance; and as it is only to true penitence that God will grant pardon, we neither feel any improvement in ourselves, nor that peace which proceeds from his favor, and hence arises our melancholy. The inference is obvious; this melancholy is our wounded self-love. But, as our Lord said to Martha, we need not be careful and troubled about many things; a strict obedience to the laws of the Gospel is the one thing needful, and in this obedience alone we shall find peace unto our souls. Let us then practice this, and calmly receive what each day brings to us. This alone can make the present scene easy to us, and this will be our best preparation for the life to come.

In proportion to the reflections of wounded pride and mortified self-love, is the peaceful calm and holy tranquility which a conscience at ease must produce: but it is not from ourselves, nor with our own powers, that we can combat sin, or resist our enemy the devil.—Vain must be all our efforts, unless we call God to our assistance. If, however, we are of a phlegmatic and melancholy disposition, and notwithstanding our sincere endeavors to fulfill our duty, still subject to desponding and mournful reflections upon ourselves, we must have recourse to regimen, and treat our malady as a distemper of the body: this it really is, and we must bear it patiently, as we submit to a fever, or any other disorder, with which it may please God to afflict us.

You must not suppose that you are forsaken of God, because you do not feel a certain kind of rapture and enthusiasm on religious subjects, or a wish to be constantly talking of holy things. The presence of God is never more truly with us, than when we are in silence, and deeply impressed with a sense of our own unworthiness. The Scripture says, "Commune with your own heart, and in your chamber, and be still." Though you do not at all times feel the influence of God upon your soul, you have no reason to complain; you have only to keep yourself in a proper state to receive it, both by doing your duty, and avoiding the sinful allurements of the world, and all voluntary dissipation. Those amusements in which passion and vanity take a share, always draw the mind from God, and render us careless in his service. But you will perhaps say, Am I to live without any relaxation or enjoyment? No, God is not a severe master; you may find many amusements which are innocent in themselves, and which will relieve your more serious occupations, without having recourse to those which are displeasing to God; and you may partake of your very amusements in such a manner as to make them also a part of God's service.

Do not let your piety assume a melancholy and austere aspect. Where the Spirit of God is, there is true liberty; if you really love God, you will habitually feel an inward content and satisfaction; but if you seek him through fear alone, you will find only constraint and alarm.

When you are conscious of any error, which separates you from God, and makes you fear to pray to him, first repent of your fault, then humble yourself before him, and receive this very terror of his displeasure as the punishment which you deserve: return with all possible alacrity to your duty, and you will by degrees regain that tranquil confidence in God's mercy, of which the sense of your faults has deprived you. Be scrupulously faithful to your stated times of morning and evening prayer. Be not discouraged if you cannot always avoid languor and involuntary absence of mind in this exercise; but endeavor to recall your thoughts to God. Persevere in what you know to be right, and walk before him in confidence and without fear. Fear contracts the heart, it is the sentiment of a slave; but hope and confidence enlarge and strengthen the soul, and incline it to that love of God, which we ought (as his children) to feel for our heavenly Father, who is ever pouring down his benefits upon us.

When you feel yourself unsteady and faint-hearted, and reluctant to obey the calls of the Holy Spirit, endeavor to strengthen your soul by the counsel and example of those who are truly virtuous; open your heart to some chosen friend, and confess your weakness; not with the desire of being flattered again into self-confidence, but that you may see and renounce your errors, and be heartily sorry for them. You must strive to conquer the resistance which your self-love makes to that humble and contrite spirit, so necessary to a Christian. Listen to God, and not to yourself. Be patient in suffering, and abundant in love towards him; speak little on sacred things, but let your actions show that the Holy Spirit dwelleth in you.

CHAPTER 11
ON SELF-KNOWLEDGE, AND THE DUTY OF SELF-EXAMINATION

It is our constant duty to examine ourselves, and to inquire strictly into the state of our hearts, towards God and our neighbor; to reflect upon it with humility, yet with confidence in God's mercy; imploring pardon for our sins and errors, and faithfully endeavoring to repair them, by our future conduct. We cannot make any more acceptable reparation for those faults into which pride or vanity may have betrayed us, than by becoming humble in our own estimation, and patiently submitting to any degradation in the sight of the world, which it may please God to appoint to us. Restrain your desires to what God chooses for you; and if you constantly make the best use of the present hour, you are sure to be prepared for those which are to follow. The duties of life are simple, and the preparation for death easy, to those who live in the habitual discharge of their duty, and in the love and fear of God. Death cannot affright them, for it brings them to the presence of their heavenly Father. Blessed are those who can say, with the royal Psalmist, "One day in thy courts is better than a thousand in the tabernacles of the ungodly."

We sin against the Holy Spirit, and wickedly try to

deceive God (not considering how impossible it is to do so), if we make any reservations in our obedience to him, or cherish any one sin, when we have forsaken the rest. We are guilty of a greater crime than that of Ananias and Sapphira, and God will not fail to punish us both here and hereafter, for so impious a desire. If we say that we have no sin, we deceive ourselves; but let us remember that we cannot deceive God; and if we impose upon the world by an outward garb of sanctity, and an appearance of holiness, while in secret we indulge any one criminal and sinful inclination, He who seeth in secret, and from whom nothing is hidden, will discover our hypocrisy, and punish us for it in that great day, when the hidden things of darkness shall be bought to light, and when we shall in vain endeavor to fly from our offended Judge.

The correction of our faults is not to be the occupation of a day, or to be compassed in the intervals of worldly amusement: it must be a work of time and patience, and demands constant watchfulness and attention. We must take care not to substitute the short and sudden impulse of a frightened conscience, for that calm and steady perseverance in amendment, which can alone succeed, and to which God has promised assistance. Establish the love of God in your heart: your life will then be holy, and your conscience clear. Pray, therefore, fervently to God, that he would give you the grace of his Holy Spirit, that you may have peace with confidence in Him, and hope in Jesus Christ.

You cannot too often look into your own heart, it is habitually full of corruption, and must be continually cleansed. It is naturally weak and prone to error, unsteady and timid towards its duties. It is so biased and occupied by its own affairs and desires, that it does not permit you to bestow sufficient thought on your fellow-creatures, their afflictions, or necessities. The fear of God, and the thoughts of death, arouse you from your worldly dream and false security, and force you to call upon him; but this sudden and short impulse is not the pure love of God, nor a real delight in his service; it is only the dread of that punishment which he has denounced against sinners; and the heart which is not continually on the watch against its own corruptions, forgets this transient glance at heaven, and returns with increased avidity to the vain pleasures of the world. You may not indeed be guilty of any great vices, such as avarice, revenge, inordinate ambition (which lead the way to monstrous crimes), and the world may give you credit for some virtues; but the love of God is not in you, and you are only withheld from these very vices, perhaps by a vague sort of fear of Him, which you can neither discard, nor explain: this is the condition against which you should be ever on the watch, and your constant prayer to God should be, to grant you a steady faith in him, and a sincere piety which may attach your soul to him, notwithstanding all the temptations of the world.

You have frequently experienced, that through precipitation and weakness, you have committed many faults, and fallen into many errors, which yet are not incompatible with a true love of God, and sincere repentance; but you do not so clearly perceive, that many more dangerous errors take their rise from a carelessness of heart, and an easy temper of mind, which does not at first appear to us as a state of sin, or a cause of displeasure to God. We may possess the principle of avarice, and our conduct may be tinged with it, even without our consciousness, because we veil it from our interior sense, by specious and plausible pretexts, and give it gentler appellations: Yet if an unexpected temptation were to attack us, we have no strong shield wherewith to defend ourselves. The same may be said concerning envy, malice, uncharitableness, and almost every other sin, to which self-interest serves as a cloak. Hence, I say, that you are full of imperfections and impurities, though your mind is truly set upon God, and your will is sincere in his service; because your will, though good, is weak, and is divided and restrained by the efforts and desires of your self-love.

Temptations must come; and those which arise from ourselves, require as much vigilance on our part, and are as painful, as those which we meet with in the world. In some respects the former are most useful to us, since by showing us the corruption of our souls, they tend to humble us in our own estimation; whereas those which arise from the world, only show us the envy, the pride, and the malignity of those about us; when, therefore, we look within ourselves, and take a fair view of the errors, and the sinfulness of our minds, we dare not, on comparison, exalt ourselves above our fellow-creatures.

If you wish to do well, pray to God for his grace, that you may be ever on your guard against the pleasing sophistry of your self-love, and the delusive opinion, to which we are all so much inclined, that we are more righteous than our neighbors. If you look only on the errors of others, you will soon learn to think yourself superior to them, merely because you are unacquainted with yourself: whereas, in order to please God, you should, by a close acquaintance with your own faults, and by a continual struggle against them, render yourself gentle and indulgent to the faults of others. You may turn your errors to your good, if you thus learn from them humility and candor. Have patience with yourself and with others; repent of your sins; deplore your own weakness, and acknowledge how unworthy you are in the sight of God. If you do this with sincerity before him, he will grant you his grace, and deliver you from your sins, by turning your heart entirely unto him, Seek not to excuse your faults; confess them to God (and to your neighbor also, if you have offended him); and bear with patience whatever blame you may receive from him. Endure the painful sense of your own infirmities, as the admonition of your heavenly Father; and assure yourself that a firm resolution to avoid the future commission of those faults, is the only way to atone for them, both to God and man.

Make use of all opportunities of leisure from worldly occupations, to recollect yourself, and to look into your account with God, without, however, relaxing in your fixed and daily intercourse with him. Let God (who is the merciful giver of all that you enjoy) be your first object; and shudder at the ingratitude of lavishing on any of his creatures, those affections which he has required for himself. Retire often, therefore, from your vain amusements, and examine your heart; remember that your God is a jealous God, and do not delay your return to him. Every moment that you willingly postpone this self-inquiry, is a criminal indulgence, and an offence to God.

Be not cast down, however, at a full and intimate knowledge of your own imperfections; nor at the repeated commission of errors, if they are but venial. We must be frail and imperfect as long as we are mortal: take care only that such errors are never willful. Turn to

God, and implore his assistance, and fear not that he will reject you, because you are not perfect. If you defer coming to God till you are free from sin, you will never approach him: god, therefore, to his holy table, and by a worthy participation of the means of salvation, you will obtain his pardon for your past failures, and the grace of his Spirit, to strive against temptation in future: and as in this world trials will come, and sin will abound, it is our part patiently to receive the one, and steadfastly to resist the other, to the end of our lives.

CHAPTER 12.
ON CHARITY, AND PEACE WITH SOCIETY

One of the greatest and most necessary virtues of this life is Charity; it is also one of the most acceptable in the sight of God, on account of its relation to our fellow-creatures. Charity, saith the Apostle, shall cover a multitude of sins: if we desire to live at peace (even with the best people), we must bear a great deal, and ask little; the most perfect of human beings is still full of imperfections. Let us set our own faults against those of our neighbors, and we shall soon find the necessity of mutual forgiveness. Happy are they, who, in bearing each other's burthens, fulfill (as the Apostle says) the law of Christ.

We cannot expect, nor even hope to pass through life in peace with each other, without the approbation and love of God; without humility, and a constant endeavor to subdue our pride and self-love. Self-love is, indeed, the root, from whence, in a greater or less degree, proceed all our passions, and the consequent mischiefs which arise to us from the indulgence of them among our fellow-creatures; it is the rock on which we too often make shipwreck of our happiness; for it is the greatest enemy to that peace with society, without which it is impossible to enjoy any comfort in this world.

In too warmly condemning the errors of others, we are guilty of a great fault; a haughty and strict severity towards their infirmities, or even their sins, shows a mind unwilling to acknowledge or perceive its own weakness. Who can say—"In their place I should have stood firm and unshaken?" Moreover, the reports which you have heard, may have exaggerated their offence, and you may have been prejudiced against them. We must, therefore, resolve to avoid all bitter speaking, all vehement expression of our sentiments towards others, and disapprobation of their conduct. We should, in general, confine ourselves to some fixed and certain rules, and beware of indulging our own feelings, or interest, in weighing the faults and errors of others: If you are really zealous for the glory of God, and think that he ought to be better served by his creatures, you will, yourself, without delay or discouragement, aspire to as much perfection in his sight, as can be the lot of humanity; and, far from beholding with rigor or impatience the errors of your fellow-creatures, you will, with a true Christian charity, seek to convince them of their faults, and to recall them to virtue; you will pray to God to grant them his grace, and to receive them into his favor. The Pharisees, who were worldly-minded men, self-satisfied, and relying on their own merits, could not endure the Publicans, who were treated by our blessed Lord with so much lenity and indulgence. The more you strive to be really worthy of the love and favor of God, the greater will be your charity, and the consequent enlargement of your heart and affections. Those who have truly renounced themselves, give themselves to God and their neighbor; and our Savior tells us, that on the love of God, and of our neighbor, hang all the law and the Prophets.

Wherefore do we desire the advantages of life so much more for ourselves, than for our neighbor?—Alas, it is through our excessive self-love. They who most ardently covet what they term Prosperity, are also always most disposed to murmur and repine against Providence, for the blessings which they see bestowed on others: and from hence arise envy, jealousy, malice, and many other evil passions, which often lead us on to commit the worst of crimes. We ought to rejoice, and be thankful to God for his blessings to ourselves; but we should also remember, that, as we are commanded by Him to love our neighbor as ourselves, so are we to rejoice in every good that arises to Him.

St. Paul has said to the Galatians, "that they should bear one another's burthens, and so fulfill the law of Christ;" but charity does not require of us that we should be blind to the faults of others; it only requires that we should not take pleasure in unnecessarily blaming our brethren, and pointing out their imperfections, rather because they do not please us, than from any desire of their reformation. We must continually remember what God has done for the vilest sinner, and that admittance into heaven is promised to all such as truly repent and forsake their sins, and moreover, you should ask yourself, when you take a pleasure in exposing the errors of others, if you are free from them?—You are much mistaken if you think so; and you would be infinitely surprised, if you were to hear yourself spoken of by those whom you so severely judge.

CHAPTER 13
ON CONTEMPT OF THE WORLD, AND THE DANGER OF EVIL SOCIETY

Let us sedulously guard ourselves against too great an attachment to our worldly possessions. If God hath given us riches, let us remember the poverty of Job, and regard them as placed in our hands, to be employed only in the service of God, through a worthy use of them; that is (after the demands which our rank and station in society make upon us) in comforting and relieving our less fortunate fellow-creatures. We may be assured that God will require from us a strict account of everything with which he entrusts us. Jesus Christ became poor for our sakes, that we by his poverty might become rich. Too much solicitude about the things of this world, is unworthy of a being who looks beyond it for his final place of rest. We should moderate our attachment to it, by considering how insecure is our tenure in it. It is our duty prudently to enjoy its comforts, and to provide, without careful solicitude, against is mischances; but let us not torment ourselves with doubts and fears for the morrow; the morrow is not ours; perhaps we may never behold it. It is our part to take care of today; and if we have our daily bread, what need have we of more? Our Savior himself tells us, "that the morrow will take heed for the things of itself;" and, "that sufficient unto the day is the evil thereof."

It is contrary to the just exercise of reason, to imagine

that there is no greater happiness intended for us, than the very imperfect and unsatisfying enjoyments of this world. But, even on the supposition that this life were all, how often should we have cause to feel and to own, that our happiness is not to be found in the good things of the world! Virtue is a greater calm to the soul, than the most precious of temporal gifts; and if we know this, and that we are incapable of prolonging (even for an hour) our enjoyment of the things of this life; should we not labor (while we yet have time) to obtain a share in that blessed inheritance which passeth not away; and which God hath prepared for them that love him, and keep his commandments?

If we are unjustly treated and slandered by the world, we should reflect that God often makes use of the crimes and wickedness of mankind to work out good to those who love and serve him. Is our fair fame torn from us, by the lying tongues of envious and malignant people? Let us console ourselves under the trial, by reflecting that God has permitted falsehood to triumph for a time, in order to show us that we are not to set too great a value on our reputation, as a means of acquiring the respect of the world; but that we are to seek first the approbation and favor of our God, and to trust in him for accomplishing the time, when the lying lips will be put to silence, and our innocence and the truth be brought to light.

To escape the corruption which the dissipation of the world and evil company produce in our souls, we must carefully avoid all confidential intercourse with those, of whatever rank in life, whose lives and manners are not in conformity to the rules and precepts of the Gospel. We are too easily seduced from our duty to God, by the maxims and conversation of the world, particularly of those who either minister to our passions, or by some agreeable qualities, first blind our understanding to their errors, and then lead us into the same faults with themselves. When it is too late, we discover the mischiefs which they have done us, and instead of retracing our steps in the road of virtue, we often plunge deeper into sin, till we fall for ever.

The Scripture tells us, that to judge of the moral and religious character of a man, we should observe who are his friends and most intimate companions; for how can they who truly love and serve God, take delight in the society of those in whom the love of God is not found, and who make his service no part of their care? A sincerely religious person cannot possibly be happy with such as do not think with the same spirit: —"Ye cannot serve God and Mammon." Our voluntary intercourse, therefore, with the wicked, will be to our destruction. It must, however, be granted, that such is the state of society, that it is not always in our power to avoid some intercourse with those who have neither piety nor religion.—This part of a man's character is often the last that comes to our knowledge, and we may have become previously connected with him; we may esteem him for some natural good qualities, we may be grateful for good offices which he has rendered us, or we may be bound to him by the ties of blood: still, however, as danger results from the pleasure which the society of such a person affords us, an intimacy with him may become hazardous to our salvation, and is, therefore, to be avoided by us as much as may be in our power; especially if we are of a weak and irresolute temper, or swayed by strong passions. In order, therefore, to keep steadily in the path of virtue, we must not only choose our friends and associates with the greatest care, but we must lay down the rule (never to be infringed upon, without absolute necessity) of commending ourselves and all our concerns unto God, and imploring his direction, mercy, and assistance, every day of our lives. This rule being regularly and strictly observed, it will be impossible for us to forget God, or to be led far astray from our duty to him. All ranks and conditions of men may find some time for this duty of daily prayer; and to those who are most apt to complain of the want of time for it, the duty is of the greatest importance. Men who are in high public station and office, and whose hours are filled up by business, are too apt to omit, from day to day, this small tribute of adoration to their Creator, and supplication for his assistance; and yet, without this assistance, no counsels or undertakings can prosper. Time is a gift from God; and he has, undoubtedly, a right to claim some portion of it for his service; enough will always remain for reasonable amusements, or relaxation from the cares and business of the world, after we have devoted that portion of it to God, which he demands of us. Let us, then, not conform ourselves to this world, but pass through it as strangers and pilgrims, seeking a better country, and following the steps of our blessed Master, who is gone before us. Let us make his precepts the rule of our conduct, and let his actions be the guide of our lives; as his death is (to all who trust in him) the seal of salvation.

To enable us to resist the temptations which the world continually offers, we should observe two rules in our conduct and practice. The first of these is, that whenever temptations assail us, we should listen to the first whispers of conscience, that faithful monitor which God has placed in our hearts, and which, if attended to, will ever prove a sure guide to us. The second rule is, at once to turn our souls to God, and to take refuge in him without doubt or fear. We cannot in all cases withdraw ourselves from temptation; but, assisted by Him, we can always fight our way courageously through it. The persuasion, that the all-merciful and all-powerful God is always present, and ready to afford us his aid under every trial and difficulty in this life, is the peculiar support of a Christian, and will be found sufficient to carry us safely through all our dangers and temptations. The Scripture says, "it must needs be that temptations come;" and that we are to account ourselves happy when we are so proved. —"My brethren, count it all joy (says St. James) when ye fall into divers temptations." And again, "My son, if thou wilt serve the Lord, prepare thy soul for temptation." Our life on earth is a warfare, both from within and from without; but if we march under the banner of Jesus Christ, we need not fear the assaults of the devil. Let us watch and pray, that we enter not (willfully) into temptation: but, if we are already beset by it, we have hope in Christ, who was himself tempted in all points, like as we are, yet without sin, and is ever able and willing to succor us, if we faithfully call upon him.

What right have you to expect happiness from the world?—Is perfection to be found among mankind?— Can you not judge by yourself, that your fellow-creatures are weak, blind, and inconstant?—that the very best of them are prone to error, and easily enticed to sin?—The world is a reed; if you lean on it, it will break under you; and (too often) its sharp point will pierce you to the heart.

You ought to despise the world, with all its allurements and concerns, in comparison with the love of God, and zeal for his service. I do not say that you are required absolutely to withdraw yourself from the world, and to renounce all commerce with it; for if you are leading an honest, sober, and regular life, you are discharging a part of your duty to God, while you are performing that which you owe to your fellow-creatures. Only let god, and not the world, have possession of your heart; you will then be secure, and instead of living in a perpetual warfare with your passions, devoured by pride, and tormented by self-love, you will act, on all occasions, with freedom and courage, and with confidence in God. Animated by a firm and well-founded hope in him, your fixed expectation of everlasting happiness will make you look with indifference on the things of this life. Make but the trail; you will soon find which state of mind is the happiest, and your own conscience must assure you which is the most safe.

The Son of God has said, that it is easier for a camel to pass through the eye of a needle, than for a rich man to enter into the kingdom of God. We are not, however, to understand these words of our blessed Lord as absolutely condemning the possession of riches, but the too frequent abuse of them by those who enjoy them. It is only by employing them to the glory of God, and the relief and service of our fellow-creatures, that we can make to ourselves friends of the unrighteous mammon, and lay up in heave a treasure that fadeth not away.

We must endeavor not to enter with too much eagerness into the transactions of the world—not to attach too much importance to what is said and done, either by ourselves or others; for this leads us into many errors, and is always the occasion of dissipating our religious thoughts, and withdrawing our souls from God. When we have ascertained how far we can serve God, or benefit our neighbor, this let us do.—So *far* is our duty; but stop there; for you will thus avoid many temptations, which would embarrass you, and, perhaps, turn you entirely away from god.—You will find it easy to observe this rule, if you accustom yourself to a constant habit of self-recollection, on every circumstance that arises, and if you never, for a moment, allow yourself to forget that you are in the presence of God. You will thus lay a powerful restraint on your passions, and tranquillize the agitation of your heart; you will recall your vain and wandering desires, your useless and weak reveries; and, by always cherishing the influence of God within yourself, you will through it enjoy a constant state of content and secularity; —and, as the Gospel tells us that a word from our blessed Lord calmed the fury of the elements, and the agitation of a tempestuous sea; so will the recollection of his presence, and the remembrance of his mercy, calm our unruly passions, and show us the path of peace and safety.

God divides this world to his creatures as it seems best to his heavenly wisdom. Some he tries by the privation of worldly enjoyments, and others by the abundance of them: but he gives his grace equally to all. If he has placed you amidst the pomps and vanities of the world, fear not; do your duty amongst them, nor suppose that you may defer seeking your Creator until you can attain a retired situation.—The idea of one day withdrawing ourselves from the world, to prepare for immortality, is a very pernicious one; and, like all other worldly hopes and plans, may never be realized. Use the present hour, if you would make your calling and election sure. You cannot arrest the strong arm of Death, or bid him wait till you have prepared yourself to obey his summons. When the Israelites were captives in Babylon, there were few of them who did not hope and expect to see Jerusalem again: and yet, how many of them resigned their breath in captivity!—How vain and illusive, therefore, were the designs of such of them as deferred the worship and service of their God, until they could adore him in the holy Temple of Jerusalem? Let us take care that we, who are so much better instructed than the Israelites were, be not still more blind.

Our blessed Lord has said to us, in his holy Gospel— "Seek, and ye shall find; knock, and it shall be opened to you." If, in order to obtain *riches,* we had merely to ask for them, what perseverance should we display! —If we had only to look for a treasure, which we were sure of finding, we should not be discouraged by any obstacles which might arise in our search after it.—If we had but to knock, to be admitted into the councils of kings, and to be invested with the highest dignities, how clamorous should we be for entrance! —Alas, what infinite trouble do men take, for the fleeting pleasures, and empty gains of mortality!—What rebuffs, what toil do we patiently endure for the phantoms of worldly glory?—Meanwhile, the treasures of heaven, everlasting life and happiness, the true and only good, are forgotten; or, if we for a moment reflect upon them, we count them as things which we shall have time enough to obtain, when we are weary of worldly enjoyments. O, blind and insensible man! Search the Scriptures, and learn from the words of our blessed Savior, that this word and all its pleasures shall pass away, but that the promises of everlasting happiness to the good, and the sentence of eternal misery to the wicked, are certain and inevitable.

"Eye hath not seen, nor ear heard, neither hath it entered into the heart of man to conceive, the joys which god has prepared for them that love him, and keep his commandments." The first Patriarchs rejoiced continually in the promises of God, and the hope of immortality, when they had no assurance of it but through faith in those promises: —And shall we, who call ourselves Christians, followers of Jesus; we, to whom all the promises have been fulfilled, by the actual coming of our Lord into the world, for our salvation; shall we prefer the vain and sensual pleasures of this life to the pure and everlasting happiness, which he has purchased for u in the life to come?—The severest trials, the most painful tortures, were not capable of making the first Christians relinquish their faith, or withdraw their confidence from God; because they knew the magnitude of those blessings which that faith held out to them: Yet we, their unworthy descendants, are ready to deny our Creator, and to disbelieve his promises, when our self-love, our luxury, or our pride, is called upon to make any sacrifices for them.

Our Savior has said, "Woe unto the world, because of offences."—How dreadful ought these words to be to those who are the followers of this world, and the partakers of its offences!—But how consoling are the same words to those who have wisely preferred the right path, and the narrow way, to the seducing allurements of a guilty world!—Again, our Savior says to his disciples, "Love not the world, nor the things which are in the world." How much reflection do these words demand from us! The world is a corrupt assemblage of irreligious and immoral men, who love nothing but themselves; or, if they have any regard for their fellow-creatures, it is not through virtue, or the love of God, but merely because they find them useful, or necessary to their own gratification. There are, indeed, many among them, who profess to have renounced the world, and to be followers of Jesus: But, alas! Notwithstanding this apparent renunciation of its follies, they preserve, in their hearts, its sinful desires, and too often break through those restraints of outward sanctity and devotion, which a wish to preserve a good reputation, and that respect, which the world (bad as it is) always pays to the virtuous, had induced them to impose upon themselves.

Our Savior has said unto his disciples, "My Peace I give unto you; not as the world giveth, give I unto you." These divine words show us how poor and contemptible a thing is this world, for which we are inclined to hazard so much. It is, in fact, but a small sacrifice which we make to our God, when we give up a sinful world for him. What weakness, therefore, is it in us, to esteem so highly, what our Redeemer has so greatly despised. We renounce the world at our baptism; but how seldom do we fulfill, or reflect on that solemn engagement!—The pleasures of the world are generally purchased with the loss of our health and fortune; but the love of God, and the service of Jesus Christ, is peace and everlasting gain. It is security to our health, and prosperity to our estate; it bridles our passions; it restrains our desires; it consoles us in sorrow; it supports us in suffering; it gives joy, even in the midst of grief; and it is not only promises, but will most assuredly bestow, unspeakable joy and happiness, to all eternity.

The contagion of bad company is more fatal to the

mind, than the casualties of the world are to the body.—
Our souls are continually attacked, through our senses;
and, without the grace of God, we should seldom be able
to resist the allurements of the world, and the
blandishments of sin, to which we are constantly
exposed.—We shall obtain this grace by a humble trust
in God, by a firm faith in his Word, and by constant and
earnest prayer, together with frequent reading and
meditating on his holy Gospel; for our best thoughts, to
be worthy of ascending to him, must be placed on his
mercy, and on the merits of our Redeemer, therein
revealed to us. Let us, then, exert all our strength, to
conquer the world and our own passions, which are our
greatest enemies. When the evil is subdued, God will
raise us above every other: We may then say with
David—"Though I pass through the valley of the shadow
of death, I shall fear nothing; for Thou art with me."

We may live in the world, without being either
devoted to it, or showing a scrupulous and haughty
contempt for its enjoyments; without being intoxicated
with its flatteries, or depressed by its misfortunes. We
may pass through it with an equal mind, holding our way
right onward, to the great end of our being (a blessed
immortality), with a tranquil mind, and steady pace,
looking upon all the works of men as known to God;
receiving the innocent pleasures which fall in our way, as
so many consolations on our journey, and looking upon
the trials which may befall us, as punishments which we
deserve.

You cannot attain true riches, until you lay them up
in heaven, where neither moth nor rust doth corrupt.
What honor or distinction can the world offer you, which
can be compared with admission into the presence of

God, and the glory of heaven?—But, in this life, the kingdom of God suffereth violence; it is continually struggling with the opposition of the devil, and the attacks of sin. It is true, you will have much to encounter from yourself, before you can become worthy of entering into the kingdom of heaven. You will experience extreme reluctance to those sacrifices, which your duty will demand of you: but God will be your support: His Holy spirit will deliver you, and you will be truly free. Your only obedience will be paid to him, and you will feel the consolation of sacrificing to your Creator your worldly attachments, and the pleasures of your self-love: you will experience the truth of those divine words of our blessed Lord—"Learn from me, of I am meek and lowly of heart, and ye shall find rest unto your souls:" you will find that inward repose and comfort which will arise from the faithful endeavor to fulfill your duty, and which you cannot enjoy amidst the vanities of sin, and the indulgence of your passions. The great point is, to establish firmly the love and fear of God in your heart: His grace will not fail to show you your errors, and to enable you to forsake your evil ways.

It is better to trust in the Lord, than to put any confidence in man. These are the words of the royal Psalmist; and every man may experience their truth. We daily put confidence in friends, who, though perhaps willing and sincere, are weak and frail; and yet we fear to trust in God. The mere promise of a man in power, fills us with delight, and gives us full security; and yet the Gospel holds out to us the promises of eternal life and happiness, unregarded! The world promises, and we believe; —God speaks, and we will not hearken. What infatuation misguides us?—What delusive phantom steps between us and our good?—O God, have pit on thy poor creatures, and withdraw this blindness from us! Give us thy grace, that we may place our whole confidence in thy mercy, and know that in the day of adversity thy help shall not fail; for Thou art from everlasting, and shalt be to all eternity.

Watch, then, and unremittingly cherish the love of God in your heart: He will be ever at hand, to enable you to stand fast against the world, and ever sufficient to support you against yourself. The vain desires of men, their inconstancy and injustice, will then appear to you as permitted and directed by the Will of God; and you will perceive, even through the deforming medium of crimes and sufferings in this world, the Wisdom, the Justice, and the Goodness of God, while this quick-passing scene, this worldly show, will be to you, only a road, and a preparation of the unspeakable happiness of the world to come.

CHAPTER 14
THOUGHTS ON DEATH

As we advance in life, and age and infirmities come upon us, the thoughts of death, and the fear of it, often take fast hold of our minds; but nothing can be more unworthy of an immortal being, than the fear of its passage to immortality, unless it arises from a deep sense of our own unworthiness.—In this case we should remember, that though the Holy Spirit has said, that in the sight of God no man living can be justified, and that before him the stars themselves are not pure; yet it also tells us, that God is merciful and good to those whose hearts are upright.—Let us beseech him to grant us this integrity of heart, which is so acceptable to him, and we may then rely on his mercy for the pardon of our sins.

When we look upon death at a distance, when, in youth, health, and vigor, we cast our eyes toward the grave, our reflections are transient, and we are unmoved by so awful a prospect: But when sickness, age, and infirmities, show us the near approaches to the tomb, our weak nature turns with horror from the idea of dissolution. It is only through faith in the promises of God, and hope in the infinite merits of our Redeemer, that we can steadfastly look on death, and overcome the terrors, which the most perfect of mortals must feel, at putting off mortality. We need not blame ourselves, if we cannot feel joy in quitting this world: Human nature cannot be perfected in this life; we may be satisfied with ourselves, if we are entirely resigned to the will of God, without murmuring or repining, when he is pleased to call for us. Death is to the best an awful summons, and human nature turns from the bitter cup; but let our spirit say with our blessed Lord—"My God, not my will, but Thine be done."

How deplorable is that blindness, which shuts the mind against the contemplation of death; although we know it to be inevitable, and that we cannot retard its approach by banishing reflection on it! The serious consideration of this awful subject would divest it of many of its terrors, and we should, by degrees, acquire the power to think of it with composure. The prospect is, indeed, terrible to us, while we are enslaved to the world, and while we place all our happiness in its enjoyments; but when we truly love God, we shall long to behold him in his heavenly kingdom. There is no way to that kingdom but by death; and though the passage from this life to the next, is awful to our mortal nature, yet God is sufficient to support us through it.—It is not from our own merits that we can derive any confidence in that hour of trial, but from a humble reliance on Him, who is our Redeemer, "who has tasted of death for us," and dispersed the darkness of the grave; even Jesus Christ, "the Captain of our Salvation:"—He has opened to us the gate of life and immortality: He himself has led the way, and is gone to prepare a place for us; and through faith in Him, and trust in his merits, we have a powerful claim to the mercy of an offended God. When we have died unto sin, in our spiritual nature, the death of the body is only the consummation of the work of grace, and the beginning of our everlasting happiness; and in our last conflict we shall be enabled to say—"O Death, where is thy sting? O Grave, where is thy victory?—Thanks be to God, who giveth us the victory, through Jesus Christ our Lord." Amen.

We strive to stifle the thoughts of death, and to banish them from our minds, in order to avoid depression and sadness; but how great is our folly in so doing?— Death will come, whether we prepare for it or not: —and when it calls upon us to bid an everlasting farewell to all our earthly pursuits and enjoyments, we shall then clearly perceive (but, alas, too late) the fatal error into which we have fallen; we shall then see, that the best use which we could have made of our talents, our health, or our riches, of our time, and of all the events of our lives, would have been to employ them as the means of preparing ourselves for death. Moreover, the habitual *consideration* of *death* is the most powerful restraint we can have on our conduct in this life—and we should keep Death in view as our only object and end.—Our Lord himself has desired us to pray for the coming of God's kingdom; which means, that we may be fit to enter into it by death; and the Apostle Paul desires all Christians to consider death as the finishing of their sorrows, and to take comfort in the thoughts of it.

In this uncertain state of being, we should always remember our Savior's words, in the parable of the worldly-minded man,—"Thou fool, this night thy soul shall be required of thee:" The, whose shall those things be, which thou hast provided?—Dreadful is the thought of death to those who are devoted to this world, and who go on, living as if they were never to die.—Alas, why do we not grow wise unto salvation?—Why do we not contemplate the rich and prosperous of all ages?—Of what avail, to them, was all their prosperity, when Death urged his irresistible claim?—What could they reply to those awful words, "Thou fool, this night thy soul shall be required of thee?" They, who are at present acting the most brilliant parts on the great stage of existence, or who are reveling in luxury, shall soon close their short scene, and be forgotten by those who succeed them; and if they have neglected to secure to themselves an inheritance in that kingdom "which fadeth not away," how improvident have they been!—The pyramids of Egypt are still standing; but of them, by whom they were built, not a trace remains. Life is of little advantage to man, unless he makes use of it to prepare for death; and thereby to secure to himself, through Christ, an entrance into the everlasting and unspeakable happiness of heaven.

Our Savior commands his disciples to take care that the light which is in them be not darkness. How vile must our faults appear in the sight of God, when even our virtues are not free from imperfection!—How ought we to tremble, when we remember that we must all appear before his judgment-seat? How idly, how carelessly do we too often perform our services to Him! With what unconcern do we talk of him, as if we were no way interested in the existence of a God!—Let us carefully look into ourselves, and, before all opportunity is lost forever, let us take care that the light which is in us, be not darkness.

"Watch, therefore; for ye know not what hour your Lord will come." These words of our Savior are addressed to men of all ranks and ages; and yet we are so occupied with our vain projects, and worldly enjoyments, that sickness, or the approach of death itself, is often insufficient to awaken our attention to them. But why are we so fond of this life, so unwilling to think of quitting this world?—Alas, it is because the love of God is not in us; and because we do not value, as we ought, the joys of heaven, or the promises of everlasting life.—O, wretched slaves of sin! whom not even a crucified Savior dying for you, lifts above the corruption of your mortal state; a state, in which, by your own confession, you are miserable,—awake from this sad delusion, before it is too late!—Watch and pray; for ye know not the hour when your souls must appear before the judgment-seat of Christ.

CHAPTER 15.
ON THE PROPER USE OF OUR TIME, AND THE DANGER OF MISEMPLOYING IT

It is not necessary to enforce the absolute *duty* of employing your time well, if you have at all learned your duty to God: But there is still much to learn, concerning the *disposal* of that which (if well used) is to lead us to immortality. It always has been, and, alas, always will be, much easier to meet with good people in theory, than in practice; but we must remember that, in the proper management of our time, nothing but constant practice is of any avail in the sight of God.

"To everything there is a season, and a time for every purpose under heaven;" that is, for everything that is good, and fitting for a Christian. We should lay it down as one essential and unerring rule, neither to waste our time in folly, nor destroy it by idleness. We too often hear the want of time pleaded in excuse for the neglect of duty; but we should find our time fully sufficient for all our occasions, if we would apportion it in a regular manner to our several duties and occupations; still, however, making our worldly cares and employments subservient to our duty to God, and to the furtherance of our everlasting hopes. From the moment in which we are capable of thought and reflection, to that in which thought and reflection cease, God will require from us an account of his most precious gift, our time. Is it not well worth our while to inform ourselves, early, in what manner we may best make use of it? We cannot be too earnest in our consideration of this subject, nor should we ever thing ourselves too young to begin it. The bible tells us to remember our Creator in the days of our youth; and to what purpose should we do this, unless to serve and please Him, by performing our duties? In that important one of regulating our time, it is not by hurry and impatience, by undertaking too many things at once, and but half-doing each of them, that we shall succeed, but by submitting ourselves, in our early years, to the experience and direction of those who are our instructors and advisers. Happy are those whose you is trained up in virtue and goodness, by religious and affectionate parents, or faithful friends; who, being sensible of the high importance of their own time, and showing, by their lives, the use of it, are at once both precept and example to those around them. Let the pure heart of uncorrupted innocence be given to God, before it is contaminated by sin, or led astray by self-love and wayward passions.

One general rule for the proper use of our time, is, to accustom ourselves to live in a constant state of dependence upon the grace of God; receiving it from him in such portions as he sees fit to bestow on us; beseeching Him to grant it to us, and endeavoring, as we grow in years, to advance in his favor; repairing (by a holy use of the present hour) our mis-spent time, and guarding against the waste of it in future. We are too much inclined to waste that time which we can never recall: We do so, not only by idleness and evil works, but by doing what may be in itself innocent, and proper for others, but with which either our situation, or our calling, has no concern. Our worldly employments need no other regulation, as to time, than the order in which Providence has placed both them and ourselves: We have but toi follow that order with obedience and punctuality, and (when God has assigned to us our post in life) to submit our desires, our humors, and our discontents, to Him; repressing the wish for changing our employments (be they what they may), and ever remembering, that we are only in this world on our road to a better. How foolish, therefore, are they who choose to stop on that road, enticed by the pleasant accommodation they may chance to meet with; or who go on their way dissatisfied with the roughness of the path, which they are treading, to return no more; and which, once passed, will so speedily and so certainly conduct them to everlasting joy and happiness, if they perform their journey as they ought.

All our worldly undertakings should be entered upon for the glory of God, and in the hope of everlasting felicity.—When once we have made choice of our station, or Providence has called us to it, we should contentedly go on our way, until Death calls us to resign our office. If our accounts are then such as we may hope will be accepted by our heavenly King, we need not be uneasy, or anxious, when we shall yield them up.

The time which is spent in diversion and amusements requires our utmost vigilance, and we should be continually on our guard, in the most innocent and even necessary relaxations. We should never cease to implore the Divine Grace, to preserve us from the subtle poison which too often lurks under the allurements of the world, and the pleasures of society, that we may partake of them without danger to ourselves, and with benefit to others.

This is particularly addressed to those who are placed in an elevated rank in life, and who have it in their power, by their words and actions, to set a good or bad example to such as are beneath them.

The time which we denominate our leisure, as being unconnected with our worldly cares, is the most agreeable to us, and may be made the most useful. Let it be set apart for recruiting our bodily strength, by innocent and laudable exercise, and our spiritual graces by prayer and intercourse with God. Much more might be said on this important subject, but our own reason must point out to us the different employments befitting our station. Let what has been said convince you, that the management of our time is not only the preparation for eternity, but will also be the passport to it.

Let us, then, make it our constant endeavor to pass through the daily business of this life with tranquility and composure; giving to the various interests and occupations with which it presents us, such consideration as they ought to claim from beings, whose inheritance is not among them; keeping our souls steadfastly fixed on that glorious country, where our patrimony lies, and submissive to the laws of that all-powerful King, whose subjects we are. When our hearts are thus right towards our Creator, we shall soon accustom ourselves to suspend the precipitate emotions of nature and of sin: Let us only make the trial with willing minds;—in doing so, we shall at first suffer from our self-love; but that suffering will soon cease, through the pious tranquility which will possess our souls.

CHAPTER 16.
OF WORLDLY DIVERSIONS AND AMUSEMENTS

We need not be scrupulous, in judging ourselves too strictly, for our participation of those diversions and amusements, which our rank or station in life makes it proper for us to enjoy. Some very good and well-meaning people consider all worldly amusements as criminal; but though their principle (in this censure) is good, they carry it too far—they overstrain our duty to God, and forget that care which he permits us to take of ourselves. Those amusements, which are in themselves innocent, and suitable to our situation in the world, are not displeasing in the sight of our merciful Creator; "who has richly given us all good things;" and who will accept our moderate and thankful enjoyment of them, as a part of our duty and obedience to himself.—We should avoid all appearance of over-strictness and singularity, for the sake also of those amongst whom we live, lest we raise in them a fear and dislike of our holy Religion, even while we profess ourselves its most zealous disciples.

A haughty, severe, and stoical deportment, and an unrelenting strictness of opinion, on the social and cheerful enjoyments of life, is far from giving a just and true conception of religion, to such as are averse from it, and devoted to the pomps and vanities of life. This severity (instead of convincing them of their errors, and recalling them to the God of mercy and goodness) may harden their minds still more, by representing the worship of God as a system of unceasing penance and mortification.—Many good, but mistaken people, too often seek to convert and reform others, by exhibiting, in their own practice, certain painful acts of self-denial. But it is not in these that true religion consists: —When used in moderation, they may, indeed, be innocent, and sometimes useful; but God is not to be served only with the words of the mouth, or the bending of the knee; it is the pure and upright heart which he requires, and with which alone he will be satisfied. With this pure and upright frame of mind, we may live in the world, without either affectation or singularity, and cheerfully conform to its customs and amusements, and yet preserve the most strict subjection to our duty to God. We should never fail to examine ourselves, whether the love of God be the first principle of our conduct, and firmly resist all temptations from the world, when they would engage our thoughts too much, and withdraw our hearts from Him. This is true religion, and the service of God—of that God, who made the world and all things in it; —and who, although a jealous God, is the God of love, who delights in the happiness of his creatures: —all other ways of serving him are but the outward forms and ceremonies instituted by bigotry and superstition.

But you will say, "How can I possibly preserve my will and intentions always upright and pure, whilst I live in a corrupt and dissipated world, with which I constantly mix?—How can I defend my heart against the torment of my passions, and the bad examples which surround me?—How can I hope to appear uncontaminated in the sight of that God, who is of purer eyes than to behold iniquity, when I am too often enticed away from him, by the hurry and tumult of society, which expose a

Christian's soul to so much danger?'

I acknowledge that the risk is great, and that it requires the most extreme vigilance to guard against it. It calls loudly for every precaution that can be taken; and therefore I recommend to your consideration the following advice:—

In the first place is to be prescribed, a constant use of regular Prayer, and of religious *reading*. I do not mean that sort of it which indulges your curiosity, or tends to make you more learned, and more capable of discoursing on religious subjects: There is nothing more vain and dangerous, than a passion for this sort of reading, which frequently leads the mind from God and his service, and turns it to the world, and its entanglements. Read, therefore, to inform yourself well of the simple and plain truths of Christianity; you will find them sufficiently clear, and far removed from all need of discussion or controversy. Read on religious subjects, not to extend your learning, or improve your talents for declamation, but in order to become better acquainted with yourself, and to form a more just opinion of your errors and sinful weakness; it is thus only you will become better by what you read, as you will then seek help in God, against yourself.

To this kind of reading, fail not to join constant prayer, and a frequent meditation on some important Article of the Christian Faith: and for this you may choose some part of the life which our blessed Savior passed on earth. After you have well reflected upon the truth and value of your subject, endeavor to apply it to your own practice, either as a corrective of your faults, or a stimulant of your virtues. Implore the grace of God upon your endeavors; and if you faithfully adhere to a daily rule of this kind, taking especial care, that if you cannot pass hours in your closet, you, at least, pass minutes there; you will find this to be one of the most effectual remedies against the seducing dangers of society, and the cares and allurements of worldly occupations; and may the grace of God enable you to persevere in this stated intercourse with him, and steadily to resist the interruptions, and perplexing calls of the world!

There is also another great help towards a godly life; —the setting apart of certain times and seasons, for a more particular examination and correction of yourself; when, by pouring out your heart, and confessing your sins to God, your mind is furnished with new strength, new grace, and fresh powers of resistance against the world, the flesh, and the devil. I must suppose that you will confine your amusements, and your commerce with society, within the bounds of moderation, uniting your great duty as a Christian, with the lesser duties of your fortune and rank in life. Even the world, bad as it is, is always ready to exclaim against those who, by too great an attachment to it, set their own duties at defiance; and those who are truly virtuous should rejoice that the world is so severe a censor, as it is an additional restraint upon their sinful passions. If your rank in the world places you in a court, and obliges you to mingle with the most brilliant and seducing scenes of life, you will still find it in your power to avoid being swallowed up in its vortex. You may, even at the most dissipated court, still love and serve your Creator, and by not preferring, and never voluntarily resigning yourself to its follies, you may preserve the true medium between a haughty and offensive deportment, and a licentious and abandoned one. By this conduct you will attach to yourself the affection of all who are truly good, and command the respect and esteem even of those who may affect to condemn your too rigid morality.

I am persuaded that, by attending to the foregoing rules, you will procure for yourself the blessing of Heaven, and in the most tumultuous and dissipated scenes of life, God will support and accompany you: You will feel the joy of his presence more delightful than all the pleasures of the world; you will act with moderation and discretion on every occasion; your commerce with others will be free from restraint, or stoical affectation; you will be (as St. Paul says) in the world, as if you were secluded from it; and yet you will lead a cheerful, easy, and pleasant life, beloved and esteemed by all who know you. If you feel your spirits depressed by affliction, or too much elevated by prosperity, you will humbly and confidently address yourself to your heavenly Father, and you will look to him for comfort, hope, and fortitude in sorrow, and for moderation and composure in joy.

CHAPTER 17
ADVICE ADDRESSED PARTICULARLY TO PERSONS LIVING AT COURT

Although you live in the splendor and luxury of a voluptuous court, yet you are far from being free; your chain of gold is often as heavy to you as a chain of iron, and you are often galled by your fetters; for, at a court, you are exposed to envy, detraction, and malignity; and your captivity is scarcely preferable to that of a person unjustly detained in a prison. The only reflection, which can give any satisfaction to a virtuous mind, is, that God has placed you there; and it is this same consideration which affords the best support under unjust imprisonment.—Thus there is but little difference in the situations, except the empty show of vanity and splendor, which, far from being of any real advantage, only exposes you to flattery and deceit. The foregoing reflection will afford you inexhaustible comfort in both these situations, and, indeed, in every other in which you may be placed; and if you are weary of the hurry and dissipation of a life at court, because you have not sufficient time to devote to God, and to cherish the thought of him in your heart; *recollect*, that, in the discharge of your duty, wherever he has placed you, you are as sure of his favor and acceptances, as if you passed every hour of your life in meditation and prayer.

CHAPTER 18.
ON TEMPTATIONS AND TRIALS IN A LIFE OF GRANDEUR AND PROSPERITY

God has appointed to every situation in life, some unhappiness, and some trial; nor are those whom he has placed in the lowest paths of mortality to suppose, that the high and splendid ranks in life are exempt from sufferings: on the contrary, in many cases, they even exceed their own. A poor man, who wants bread to eat, and a house to shelter him, may (in his extreme poverty) envy those, whose exalted station and worldly comforts appear to him secure happiness; but could he view these objects of his envy, divested of that vain parade which dazzles his eyes, he would cease to repine. Thus we must confess, that Providence is more impartial in its earthly distributions, than our impatience and discontent, under its various trials, are willing to allow. It holds the cup of calamity to all human beings, at some period of their lives; the very dregs of that cup are often appointed to royalty; for neither the splendor, nor the magnificence of a throne, is a shield against misfortune. God thus declares his sovereignty over all mortal power, and asserts his own right over the creatures whom he has made.—Happy are they who look upon this sublunary scene with the eyes of a pure heart (as St. Paul says), and who are ready to acknowledge, that "favor is deceitful, and beauty is vain;" and to remember, that "the fear of the Lord is the beginning of wisdom."

Afflictions are not all the trials of this life; God's grace is often more necessary to us in prosperity than in adversity. Without it we are ever prone to evil, and are led away by every folly and temptation. We have too much reason to apply to ourselves the words of our blessed Savior to his disciples,—"The spirit truly is willing, but the flesh is weak."

Hear me, O my God, when I call unto Thee!—Grant to us, thy poor sinful creatures, Grace that we enter not into temptation; or, being entered into it, save us from sin, and recall us to thyself, through Jesus Christ our Lord.

CHAPTER 19.
FAMILIAR LETTERS ON RELIGIOUS SUBJECTS

You have shaken off your dependence on God, and you have forgotten your Christian duty, through your excessive anxiety about your worldly affairs. This is the great cause of your present unworthy life. You have lived without God, and you have trifled away that precious time, which you ought to have devoted to the advancement of your everlasting happiness, on what has no more durable existence than a spider's web. Consider how soon the hand of death may, in one moment, dissolve all your worldly projects; consider, that if you have not sought God in this world, you cannot expect to find him in the next.—Reflect seriously on your own situation, return to god, and let your over-anxiety cease. Remember, that the disposal of all things is entirely in his hands, and that, were you even to succeed in your designs, unless you submit yourself, and all that belongs to you, to his Will, you cannot ultimately prosper. Have recourse to your Creator; seek him by prayer and repentance: —If he does not grant you the return of that happy tranquility and confidence in him, which you once enjoyed, remember that you have deserved his displeasure, by suffering the vanities of the world to withdraw your thoughts from him, and call upon his mercy, through the merits of your blessed Savior:

Persevere in the path which he has pointed out to you; you will then find rest to your soul in this life, and you may look forward, with hope and trust, to eternal joy in the life which is to come.

Discretion is a very necessary qualification towards a holy life; but you will not so easily acquire it by a continual restraint over yourself, as by a habit of silence, and an absence of curiosity for everything which does not materially concern you: You must not, however, carry this habit so far, as to show a morose and cynical disposition in your intercourse with society. There is a medium in all things; and it should be the study of your whole life to attain it. Prudence in our commerce with the world, is as necessary to our comfort in it, as it is to our virtue; but we can only acquire it by putting our trust in God, and by constantly referring all our concerns to him, and imploring his Holy Spirit to guide us. We may then trust our own powers; because they will then be under his direction.

However solid your understanding, and strict your principles may be, yet, if you are naturally of an ardent and lively disposition, you will be perpetually in great danger from the temptations of the world; you will conceal your self-love with the fair disguise of heroism and generosity, and, led away by the *semblance* of virtue and worth, in the objects which engage your feelings, you will overlook the reality. This will expose you to severe trials, and frequently (if you are not on your guard) to much error: It will also make you appear greatly inferior to many who have not half your sense. You will, in many cases, be very clear-sighted in the affairs of others, yet have no discretion in your own; and your thoughts will be continually wandering after every folly that approaches you under an attracting form. While you are thus involved in error yourself, you will be apt to suppose your favorites gifted with virtues and good qualities, which they do not possess, merely because they have, by some pleasing charm, rendered themselves agreeable to you. By the same fascination, you may be led to follow their vicious examples, because your judgment will be overpowered by your feelings. There is but one remedy for you: —Distrust yourself, calm the ardor of your passions, examine well the things which you find so attractive, and pray to God for the direction of his Holy Spirit. If you will but as sincerely endeavor to please God, as you do to please the objects of your attachment, you will then enjoy a blessed tranquility. Pray, therefore, to God, to moderate your expectations from the world, and you attachment to even laudable qualities in your fellow-creatures, when they induce you to neglect your duty to him. From the want of this precaution it arises, that you are so often disappointed in the characters of your associates; but here, too, you forget that your own is, perhaps, as imperfect. You must accustom yourself, therefore, to judge with more impartiality of others, and to expect less from them; and when you find great errors, or even vices, in those with whom you are connected, do not give way to disgust and disdain for them: Remember the merciful forbearance of our blessed Lord, who has told us, that he came not to call the righteous, but sinners to repentance. Be quiet and patient with them; advise them gently for their good; God will give a blessing on your endeavors, and the efforts which you make in favor of your fellow-creatures will turn to your own happiness. He who strives to reclaim a sinner from the error of his ways, shall find it revert in blessing to his own soul; for

Charity shall cover a multitude of sins.

You have many good qualities, but I wish you to possess many more; and, believe me, it is in your own power to acquire them. Begin by correcting those failings which you are too apt to indulge; particularly that extreme attention which you give to outward appearance, while you are careless of the motives from which your actions spring. Accustom yourself to pause, and examine the lively, and, too often, uncontrolled emotions of your heart: place them before God, and try them by his laws: and let your haughtiness of disposition, your rigid attention to the opinions of the world, your taste for grandeur and show, your severity against all irregularity in the conduct of others, be duly submitted to the rules of the Gospel, and you will then be on your guard, and armed against yourself.—Use prayer as your constant help and resource, and let the experience of your own weaknesses teach you compassion towards those of others; for our Savior himself has told us, "that with what judgment we judge, we shall be judged." You are scrupulously attentive to the superficial virtues, which appear to the world; I would wish you to pay more regard to those which are pleasing to your God. Leave the world alone; what has it done for you, in comparison of Him to whom you owe your existence?—You fear God more than you love him; you hope to satisfy him by a ceremonious observance of forms, instead of that unstudied and willing obedience, which flows from confidence and affection, and in which alone he delights. Let us not make a compromise with our sins, or place them in reserve between us and our God; let us give them up at once; it is the only way to find rest for our souls. Let us support our spiritual nature by prayer for the grace of the Holy Spirit; for, as our corporeal frame requires frequent supplies of nourishment, so have we need, by frequent prayer, to refresh and strengthen that better part of us, which is to survive to all eternity.

Your good dispositions and great talents will but render you more criminal in the sight of God, unless you use them as you ought; for where much is given, must will be required. Remember that you fail in your duty, whenever you hesitate to sacrifice to God even the most cherished and valuable of his gifts, if he thinks fit to reclaim them. The service of God, and our duty to him, does not consist in fine sentiments or long prayers, or in ostentatious acts of charity, but in the inward man, the secret spirit, and the desire of our hearts, from whence proceeds a pure and holy life. You are not placed in this world to enjoy constant happiness, nor to please yourself. St. Paul tells us, that even our blessed Savior, who is Lord of all, "sought not his own pleasure," and "came not to be ministered to, but to minister." Shall we, then, dare to murmur, when we are called upon to follow his example, in resigning or suffering, according to the will of our heavenly Father?

If you are called to an office, which invests you with authority over others, you must be doubly watchful over yourself. The more conspicuous is your situation, the more perfect you should become, both for your own sake, and for the sake of those who look up to you. There is no instruction so efficacious as a good example, no authority so secure, as that which is softened by it; for if you practice what you enforce, there can be no murmurs against you. Begin by your own actions, and your words will be attended to on all occasions. Words alone are often of no effect, but example speaks to the heart. Be yourself the most humble and patient, the most contented and obedient, the most docile and regular, of all whom you govern; obey yourself the regulations which you have made, and the laws which you prescribe, if you desire to have them obeyed by others: or, rather, let the obedience of those under you be paid, not to you, but to those laws, and be yourself the first to submit to them. Flatter no imperfection in those who are under your care, but endure patiently all their infirmities. Do not discourage the weak, by praising and upholding the more enterprising. The more necessary you may find your authority, the more you should tempter it with moderation and gentleness. If the yoke of our blessed Savior is easy over us, miserable sinners, how can we venture to show an unrelenting severity towards our fellow-creatures?—It is by overcoming yourself that you will obtain grace to govern and overcome the minds of others: you must learn to endure, before you can be endured, and to love, before you can be beloved.—Be solicitous to make yourself acquainted with the dispositions of those who act under you, and endeavor to supply their wants, rather than o excite their admiration, or to dazzle their understanding; show them a sincere heart, and let each one know by experience, that he will find consolation and security, in opening his mind to you. When you are obliged to correct, let it be with gentleness and reluctance; yet fail not to reprove when it is necessary to do so; but do it with an air of kindness, and not with asperity. Let none fear to be deceived in trusting you; be not hasty in your decisions, but when once made, let them be irrevocable. Do not lose sight of any individual, nor be careless of the interests of those who do not happen to please you; maintain a strict impartiality on every occasion, listen with gratitude and patience to those who are sincere enough to tell you of your faults, and do not let them find this mark of regard for you injure them in your estimation; in short, correct and overcome yourself, and submit yourself to God and to his holy laws, before you pretend to make others submit themselves to yours. You must have a regard to the different dispositions of those under you, and where you meet with an ungrateful soil, do not expect as much from it as from more gentle spirits: not that you must weaken or relax the laws for them, but you must, on some occasions, tolerate and overlook what it might endanger your authority to notice with severity. You must wait, you must hope, you must entice refractory and seditious minds towards you, before you *punish*. God gives his blessing to this merciful and paternal conduct, and will assist you to turn the hearts of those over whom you rule; and where the blessing of God is not, there can be nothing but anarchy and confusion: —seek, therefore to deserve his blessing, and you will govern in peace.

Great talents are the gifts of God, and are, therefore, highly to be valued; but the pride with which they too often inspire their possessors, is extremely dangerous. It would be much better for you to be poor and ignorant, and satisfied with those around you, than to have superior abilities, and to look down with scorn on those, whose merits and talents you think inferior to your own. Your qualifications, however extraordinary, are not your own work; and if you pervert them, they will only turn to you own condemnation, and double your guilt in the sight of God. Think less of your learning, your wit, your taste, your science, and your attractions, and pray to God to add humility, and all the Christian virtues, to your character; for, without these, your brightest talents can only serve to dazzle the world, but will avail nothing to your own salvation.

You complain of the solitude in which you live, and the want of occupation which you find in your seclusion from the world; but you should not allow discontent and idleness to invade your present salutary retirement; contrive innocent amusements for yourself, and seek out occasions of doing good: you can never fail to meet with opportunities of being useful to your fellow-creatures, while you live among them: Your days may seem long and heavy, yet how swiftly does time *really* pass on, never to return! You may make for yourself a happy retrospect of the hours which you now find so wearisome, if you fill them with useful and virtuous actions. Cease, then, to regret that you are at a distance from the more brilliant scenes of life, and the dissipation of society; recollect, that there you would be more exposed to temptation; you would hear more idle talking; you would mix with many vain and contemptible characters; you would be more exposed to the snares of vice, and the contagion of bad example; you would be liable to the attacks of envy, and the sneers of pride; you would commit many faults, which you may escape in retirement, and you would have much self-reproach to endure. You might, indeed, live in greater enjoyment of sensual pleasures; but then your expenditure would be in proportion, and your vanity would too often endanger your prudence; and, above all, it is too probably, that you would scarcely bestow a thought upon your God, upon death, or upon your salvation. Is it not much better to pass your short term in this life without constant indulgence and gratification, than to hazard your eternal happiness in the next. The world offers only vain pleasures, and they are mingled with many pains, and our tastes must be sadly depraved, if we much regret the absence of its sensual delights.

I have lived among the rich and powerful, have been caressed by the great, and stood high in the favor of royalty: I have been flattered, surrounded with splendor, and courted in society; yet I inwardly rejoice that the day is at length arrived, when, by a prudent retirement, I am left to myself. Be satisfied with your present retreat, do your duty in it, and detach your thoughts from the pomps and vanities of this perishable life. You describe your sentiments to me so strongly, that I perceive god has touched your heart; take care that you shut it not against his Holy Spirit. If you seriously desire to reform, and to be worthy of his favor, you must begin with your inward self; your passions, you vain desires, your delicate tastes, and all your selfish delights, must be submitted to the laws of God, and the rules of the Gospel. If the spirit of prayer, and the love of God, has entered into your soul, you may then rejoice, for you have found the hidden treasure, the heavenly manna, which is to be your everlasting support; you will have no tormenting fears for futurity, no discontents at the present scene; you will view the infinite goodness and Love of God, providing constantly for your necessities, and ordering all things that befall you for your real good. Make but trial of this state, and endeavor sincerely to deserve the benefits which each day brings to you, and God will not fail to perform all his promises.

When a seducing remembrance of past pleasures, or an overwhelming recollection of past sorrows, seizes your mind, humble yourself before God, worship Him, and submit to his holy Will; neither nourishing the dangerous recollection of your errors, nor rebelling against his chastisements. It is more easy to live a life acceptable to God, than we generally suppose: Pray for the grace of God, which is never denied to the repentant sinner, and resign yourself to its influence: you may thus, even on earth, partake of the joys of heaven, by doing the will of your Creator. O, blessed state of peace and security! How preferable to the empty pleasures of the world!—this was what St. Paul desired for the faithful, when he wished them to be in the bowels of Jesus Christ.

You ought to make it one of your chief duties, to keep a restraint on the words of your mouth, and to regulate your tongue, and (as far as the claims of society will permit) to keep silence, as a security. A habit of prudent silence allows our thoughts to rest with God, spares us many sinful and foolish words, and avoids much danger to ourselves, and injury to our neighbor, in slander and defamation: Silence humbles the mind, and detaches it from the vain concerns of life; it also affords a great addition to our time; for if you make it a rule, neither to speak uselessly nor wickedly, you will have your thoughts at liberty, many times, even in the midst of company; and though you may be in a situation, where you are obliged to mix much with society, still, if you cannot give whole hours to God, fail not to give him half-hours, or even minutes; and this fidelity to Him, in all you can spare from the calls of life, will (even in its smallest portions) be as acceptable in the sight of God, and procure as much of his favor, as if you devoted whole hours to him, from a life of more leisure, and more free from the claims of the world.

You should always distrust any of those apparently good qualities, which you meet with among your acquaintance, when you perceive that they are founded upon self-confidence, and self-love. The Gospel says— "That which is highly esteemed among men, is often an abomination in the sight of god;" for God knoweth the heart, and to Him the purity of its motives is alone acceptable. Sins committed through passion, weakness, or ignorance, are less offensive to God, than the vain-glorious, worldly virtues, on which men pride themselves, without bestowing a thought upon their Creator. Forbear, then, to estimate the characters of your fellow-creatures by your own false judgment, and depraved ideas of grandeur and goodness. You may be assured, that there is nothing really good or great in humanity, that does not humble itself in the dust, and bow before the throne of our heavenly King, acknowledging there its weakness and infirmity.

CHAPTER 20.
ON MARRIAGE

Marriage was instituted by God himself, between our first parents, in the happy state of innocence, and in the blissful dwelling of Paradise: it is, therefore, of high and sacred origin: Jesus has sanctified it, by performing his first miracle at the marriage at Cana; he thereby manifested his approbation of it. The wisdom and goodness of God has provided for the peace and comfort of his creatures, by this institution, as a bar against the anarchy and confusion which would otherwise prevail, even in the most refined society. The sacred bond of Marriage is too often ridiculed and deprecated, by the libertinism of youthful passions; but it is the most perfect state of happiness which this life affords, provided it is entered upon wisely, and supported with mutual indulgence and affection. St. Paul has left us some admirable instructions on this state, and has clearly proved the holiness of a virtuous union, and the favor which it finds in the sight of God.—"Husbands, love your wives, even as Christ also loved the Church, and gave himself for it: so ought men to love their wives as their own bodies: He that loveth his wife, loveth himself; for no man ever yet hated his own flesh, but nourisheth it, and cherisheth it, even as the Lord the Church. Let every one of you, in particular, love his wife even as himself; and let the wife see that she reverence her husband."

By the sacred tie of marriage, two persons are made one in their interests, affections, and every worldly consideration; and they are also one in the sight of God. To make this sacred tie productive of mutual comfort, it must not be lightly contracted, nor the state entered upon without due reflection on the characters which are to be united; and even between those whose characters appear the most likely to ensure happiness in marriage, there must be a constant regard to each other's wishes and inclinations, as well as a constant indulgence towards each other's faults and weaknesses. Let the husband cherish and protect his wife; let him show her, at all times, that he prefers her to all other women; let him ensure the submission of her will to him, by gentleness, persuasion, and tenderness, and not by arbitrary authority; let him communicate his affairs to her with confidence, since, by marriage, all his concerns become equally hers; and let him teach her to find pleasure in the domestic cares of his family, and the management of his children, by sharing them with her.

Nor are the duties of a wife less important to their mutual happiness, or less absolute on her part. Let her love her husband next to her God; let her submit to him with mildness, and obey him with cheerfulness; let her deserve his confidence by her discretion, her modesty, and reserve; and let them both be inviolably faithful to each other; not content with turning with horror from actual alienation, but even avoiding, with the utmost precaution, everything which may create the least jealousy or uneasiness to each other, or break that confidence, which is the bond of their union, and which, once broken, or weakened, cannot be restored.

CHAPTER 21.
ON THE HABIT OF CONFESSING OUR SINS
TO GOD

The Scripture tells us, that "if we confess our sins to our heavenly Father, he is faithful and just to forgive us our sins, and to cleanse us from all unrighteousness."— Nothing tends more to inspire us with horror against sin, and with a spirit of humility, than a habitual examination of ourselves, and a sorrow for our sinful errors before God: but we must make no intentional reserves in doing this: the heart is at all times known to God; we cannot possibly conceal anything from his knowledge, and the intention of doing so is, therefore, as useless as it is sinful. Lay aside all your self-love, when you enter into the presence of God, and remember that you intercourse with your Maker must not be that of stated and ceremonious addresses; you must open your heart before him, as a child to its father, and perform his will with ease and simplicity.

CHAPTER 22.
ON PERSEVERANCE IN WELL-DOING

If once you permit your own will to obtain the victory over any known duty, you will never attain to any excellence. A strict and steady perseverance in well-doing, can alone procure for you the favor of God. We are always too much inclined to hear ourselves upon every occasion, and to shut our ears to the calls of duty. God alone directs the hearts of all men; pray to him, therefore, to purify your heart, and to turn towards you the hearts of others.—"Except the Lord keep the city, the watchman waketh but in vain."—If you suffer the allurements of the world to draw you aside from God and your duty, and to banish him from your thoughts, you are a thousand times more criminal than if you had never known him. God demands from us as much perfection in this life, as our nature will admit, and he commands us to labor unceasingly for it. Jesus himself said to his disciples—"Be ye therefore perfect, as your heavenly Father is perfect:" and our blessed Lord has taught us to pray that the will of God may be done on earth, as it is in heaven. We are all invited to this state of perfection; but how few, alas, endeavor to attain it!—Be sober, be vigilant in the performance of your duty, and do not follow the example of the ungrateful Israelites, who, being sustained by God with manna in the Wilderness, murmured against his goodness, because they had not also the flesh-pots of Egypt.

CHAPTER 23.
ON GOOD WORKS

Our salvation is not to be the price of leading a harmless life on earth, and only abstaining from what we know to be evil. The kingdom of heaven is not to be so easily entered; nor will those be truly acceptable in the sight of God, who only pay him the obedience of a slave, and who observe his laws, only through fear, and the dread of punishment. God requires from us the love of free-will, the service of choice, the obedience of content and pleasure. God has told us, that we are to serve him by religious action, and by being useful in the world; and this we must do, if we are sincere in our love for him. Many people, who mean well, deceive themselves on this point, and suppose that, though they fail to perform good works, they will be saved by faith alone; that is, if they steadfastly believe, and do not commit any great sin. It would be easy to undeceive them, if they would but examine into this subject. Their error is a very dangerous one, and arises from false ideas both of God, and of themselves. They are jealous of their liberty (as they call it), and they fear to lose it, by being too zealous in the service of God: but let them search the Scriptures. St. Paul says, "Know ye not that your body is the Temple of the Holy Ghost: and, "Ye are not your own, for ye are bought with a price; therefore glorify God in your body, and in your spirit, which are God's." We belong to God, he having made us, not for ourselves, but for his own glory; and he has an absolute right to our obedience and service. We have not (properly speaking) even the right of giving ourselves to God; for we have no right whatsoever over ourselves: and therefore, if we do not acknowledge that we belong to God, we are guilty of a sort of religious treason, and we overthrow the order of Nature. We cannot possibly question the right which God has to impose laws upon us, nor that it is our part to obey them; how can we, then, imagine that we are to be saved by a mere barren faith, without that obedience which those laws require of us?—If we had written the Gospel ourselves, we should, no doubt, have taken care to adapt its precepts to our sinful deficiencies; but God did not consult us, when he ordained it to be the rule and guide of our lives. He has given us no hopes of salvation, but through implicit obedience to his commands; an obedience which he enables us to perform by his strengthening grace; therefore the Gospel tells us, that faith without works is dead.—Was not Abraham justified by works, when he offered up his only son Isaac upon the altar?—For, as the body, without the spirit, is dead; so faith, without works, is dead also. This is the Law which is set before us; it is of the same force to all ranks and conditions of men; and no man may add to it, or diminish from it.

We often say that we desire to be instructed how we are to advance in the path of virtue; but, alas, these are too often but idle words; for when we have gained the knowledge "how we are to walk, and to please God," we do not always use it to that end. We cannot but feel our own sinful state, and we are willing to persuade ourselves, that it is enough for us to say that we wish to be saved: but let us not deceive ourselves in a matter of such importance; vain and inefficacious are all our words and wishes, if we do not accompany them with good works, and a total sacrifice of ourselves; and we are commanded in Scripture, not only to inquire into the Will of God, but to do it, ascribing all that we thus do, not to ourselves, but to God. These, and these alone, are the conditions of eternal life.

Woe be to him, who, as a minister of the Gospel, will dare to soften, or to explain away its laws, for the sake of pleasing worldly-minded men. The ministers of the Gospel are not the founders of it; they are not, therefore, answerable for its severity; and at their own peril be it, if they deceive those to whom it is their duty to preach it. The laws of the Gospel will judge them more strictly than other men; forasmuch as it is their duty to understand, and to expound them faithfully to their fellow-creatures. Woe to the ignorant, cowardly, or flattering preacher, who seeks to enlarge the strait path of duty; for wide is the gate, and broad is the way that leadeth to destruction. Let the pride of man be silent; let him bear the yoke of the Gospel, and pray to god for that grace and assistance to obey his laws, which is promised to all those who ask it with a sincere and humble heart.

CHAPTER 24.
ON SIMPLICITY, OR SINGLENES OF HEART,
AND ITS EFFECTS

There is a kind of simplicity which is worldly, and which, among men, is accounted a fault: there is another sort of simplicity, which is a heavenly virtue. We condemn that simplicity which consists in a want of discernment, or an ignorance of people and things; and when we have occasion to speak of this quality, we always represent the person to whom it belongs as credulous, weak, and silly. That simplicity which is a virtue, far from being weak, or blind, is something celestial and sublime. All those who are virtuous, know and feel what it is; they admire and esteem it in others; they are sensible when they hurt or offend it, and they wish to possess it themselves; yet they find it hard to describe what it is, what are its attributes, and in what it consists. It is that rare quality of the soul, which the Scripture calls singleness of heart. This heavenly simplicity is an uprightness of mind, which seeks no crooked paths in the discharge of its duty, no fond applauding gratification of vanity and self-love, but performs its various duties for the approbation of God alone: it is a higher virtue than sincerity, and of a different kind. Many are sincere, without possessing this simplicity. The sincere man will say nothing that he does not believe to be true, and he desires to pass only for what he really is; and he is ever studying, and examining himself, lest he should get credit with the world for what he is not. These are the distinguishing marks of sincerity; but a man may act and feel in this manner, and yet not possess the least of true and heavenly *simplicity;* —and though sincerity is a great virtue, yet, when it is not accompanied (at least in some degree) by simplicity, it often degenerates into very unamiable qualities; it becomes oppressive, teasing, precise, and constrained, with others; it is not at ease with them, nor they with it; and we imperceptibly feel that we should love those better, who were less rigidly true, less exactly *good*; because we are ourselves so full of imperfections. True simplicity, or singleness of heart, will give us a just and proper degree of devotion to our God, and of attention to our duties in this world: it will prevent us from giving to any unworthy object the first place in our affections; and yet the influence which our natural and social ties have upon our hearts, will preserve us from that unbending and unfeeling stoicism, that intolerance of our fellow-creatures, which is apt to tincture a sincere and religious disposition, when there is no indulgence of the gentler affections.

If we would wish our dearest friend to be so simple, and so free in his intercourse with us, that he should even forget himself, and his own self-love, how much more do we owe this resignation, and (if I may so express it) *abandonment* of ourselves to God, who is our truest and most compassionate Friend and Father? Use, therefore, your utmost exertions to attain this rare and divine quality, which is so acceptable in the sight of God. You

149

are, perhaps, at present, far from possessing it: —no matter; let this be only an additional reason for your endeavors after it: Pray earnestly for the grace of God, and, assisted by it, you need not despair. Alas, the greater number of those who bear the name of Christians, are neither simple nor sincere, towards God or their neighbor; nor even toward themselves. The Psalmist says, that all men are naturally deceitful; and it is but too true. Even those, in whom ingenuousness and sincerity make the fairest show, have yet, in the bottom of their hearts, a secret pride and a tender and delicate self-love, which is ever striving against that open confidence, that plain, true, and clear character of the soul, in which consists simplicity, or the constant sacrifice and oblivion of ourselves.

But you will say, How can I avoid self-love?—A crowd of feelings and reflections press on my heart, and tyrannize over my mind, and produce in me a deep sensibility. This may be true; and I do not mean to exact of you more than you are able to perform; I only require that you will not cherish your self-love, nor voluntarily indulge this sensibility: If you earnestly endeavor to subdue it, you will at length succeed, you will conquer your vain and worldly desires, and give yourself entirely unto God by a sincere and perfect resignation of all your interests, your pleasures, your affairs, your reputation, and your life, into his hands, and you will contentedly receive, and hold them from him, in whatever manner he sees it fit to dispense them to you. You will not be led to forget him, if he is pleased to bless you with prosperity; nor will you be guilty of sinful discontent, or immoderate sorrow, if he visits you with trial and affliction. This alone is the free state of the soul with its Maker, and this state produces in it a perfect and true simplicity.

It is not enough that your dispositions are good, unless you put them into constant practice, without which they will never be of any real use or value either to yourself or others. You must endeavor to correct your faults, without being impatient with yourself, though you should often fail in your best purposes: Let such failures only render you more humble in your own eyes, and more compassionate towards your fellow-creatures, more upright and sincere, more innocent and ingenuous in your conduct towards them. By these means, you may hope to attain that divine simplicity, or singleness of heart, which the holy Scripture describes, and requires, and by which your soul will become ingenuous, pure and innocent, gentle towards others, and happy in itself.

CHAPTER 25.
ON THE IMPORTANCE OF WHAT WE CALL TRIFLES

You say you are often ashamed to let others know the trifling occupations which employ your days: Why are you not, then, also ashamed to give up your time in that manner?—How inconsistent must your conduct appear, even to yourself, if you will bestow on it a moment's consideration?—You dread the contempt of the world, and you do not fear the displeasure of your God!—If your occupations (however trifling) are in themselves innocent, and suitable to your station in the world, you need not be ashamed of them; and those who may despise you for them, are unworthy of your consideration. Moreover, your character appears more clearly in the manner of performing these humble duties, than in the greater actions of your life; over which (as they are subject to the eye of the world) you have, therefore, a greater guard. Be ever on your guard against pride; distrust what the world calls glory, which is the more dangerous, as it is the more attractive.—Be gentle, patient, compassionate towards your fellow-creatures, incapable of malice and uncharitableness: —"Charity hopeth all things, is not puffed up, but condescends to those of low estate." May you become dead indeed unto sin, and alive unto God; for the grace of his Holy Spirit is the true nourishment of the soul.

CHAPTER 26.
ON TRUE LIBERTY OF SOUL

When we have (as far as we are able) got the mastery over our passions, and learned to subdue our self-love, then, and then only, we enjoy true liberty of soul. Self-love is the principle of almost all our faults, and from which most of our actions spring. If you labor to subdue it, you cut up the root of many vices; and by following the precepts of Jesus, Christians will feel the truth of these words of the Apostle: —"Where the Spirit of the Lord is, there is liberty." God, then, dwells within us, and around us, and we are at peace with ourselves, although humbled through the sense of our infirmities. We then feel, that we should prefer death to the voluntary commission of a crime, and that the approbation of the whole world is of no value in our eyes, compared with the favor of God. If we meet with unkindness and contempt from the world, we remember the trials and the contempt, which our blessed Savior suffered in it. As for the trials which we receive from God, let us remember that, because they come from him, we have full reason to believe they are intended for our good, and that we are to accept them with submission, and endure them with constancy. This victory over our self-love once attained, we experience such comfort of soul, that, through faith in

God, we are capable of any suffering, and an sacrifice, which he may think fit to appoint for us. To secure, therefore, the liberty of our souls, we must remain always with our God, and follow his guidance, like little children—"of such" (and of those who resemble them), our blessed Lord assures, "is the kingdom of heaven." You are not, then, under any necessity to reflect much, nor to reason deeply on your duty; the obedience of a little child is all that is required of you. In this your soul will find its *rest*, and enjoy its true and perfect liberty; even that liberty with which Christ has made us free, and which the Scripture calls, "the glorious liberty of the sons of God."

CHAPTER 27.
CONCLUSION

What, then, shall we render unto our God, for all his mercies!—for the manifold blessings of this life, and for the blessed hope of life eternal through our Redeemer, Jesus Christ? Can we ungratefully make ourselves our first object, and this world our resting-place, when we owe ourselves to God, and have in prospect that better world, for which he has created us? Let us, then, be grateful for all his mercies; and may it please him to touch our hearts with that pure love of Him, which can give us (even in this life) a foretaste of the life to come. Let us resign ourselves to this blessed state with joy, patiently waiting, till it shall be made perfect in heaven, to all eternity. *Amen.*

ABOUT THE AUTHOR

Francois de Salignac de la Mothe-Fenelon, 1651-1715, was an important post-Counter-Reformation figure in France. He was a Roman Catholic archbishop, theologian of great sensitivity to biblical principles, and an eminent poet and writer. Much of his effort was devoted to the cause of preaching to Protestants in an effort to bring them back into the Roman Catholic fold. He was also deeply committed to efforts to apply biblical principles to the secular life. While a tutor to the grandson of Louis XIV, Fenelon wrote a scathing thinly veiled critique of the doctrine of the divine right of absolute monarchy. This work, The Adventures of Telemachus, Son of Ulysses, became one of the most popular works of the century throughout Europe. Fenelon's view angered the King who in retribution confined Fenelon to his archdiocese. In time, Fenelon was also rebuked by Pope Innocent XII for his unorthodoxy. Nevertheless, Fenelon continued to enjoy the respect and affection of his contemporaries, including members of the royal household. He is remembered today as a true member of the One Holy Universal Christian Church, a faithful Roman Catholic, a reformer, and a champion of human rights. Of our common bond of humanity, Fenelon writes:

"A people is no less a member of the human race, which is society as a whole, than a family is a member of a particular nation. Each individual owes incomparably more to the human race, which is the great fatherland, than to the particular country in which he was born. As a family is to the nation, so is the nation to the universal commonweal; wherefore it is infinitely more harmful for nation to wrong nation, than for family to wrong family. To abandon the sentiment of humanity is not merely to renounce civilization and to relapse into barbarism, it is to share in the blindness of the most brutish brigands and savages; it is to be a man no longer, but a cannibal"—from Fenelon's Dialogue des Morts (1718), quoted in Paul Hazard, The European Mind, 1680-1715 (1967).

www.ingramcontent.com/pod-product-compliance
Lightning Source LLC
Chambersburg PA
CBHW060252050426
42448CB00009B/1621